WHY EVERY AMERICAN SHOULD JOIN THE MILITARY

WHY EVERY AMERICAN SHOULD JOIN THE MILITARY

AMERICA'S HIDDEN SECRET TO SUCCESS

DELANO JOHNSON

HOUNDSTOOTH
PRESS

WHY EVERY AMERICAN SHOULD JOIN THE MILITARY
America's Hidden Secret to Success

FIRST EDITION

ISBN   978-1-5445-4517-2 *Hardcover*
          978-1-5445-4516-5 *Paperback*
          978-1-5445-4518-9 *Ebook*

This book is dedicated to:

...Everyone who ever believed in me, gave me motivation when it was needed, prayed for me when I was deployed to Afghanistan, prayed for me before and after Afghanistan, loved me past my flaws, loved me when I wasn't easy to love, helped groom me into the man I am today, taught me lessons worth more than any material possession, fought for me when I wasn't able to fight for myself, checked me when I needed to be checked, brought me joy, challenged me to think outside the box, taught me the value of having a relationship with God, and loved Lano for Lano. My heart would put the names of every single individual I feel deserves recognition but my PTSD won't let me; therefore, I'll simply put titles. Thank you, Momi, Daddy, Baby Girl, Chinu, Big Bro, Big Sis, my grandmothers, my grandfathers (RIP), brandi, my aunties, my uncles, my nieces, my nephews, my cousins, my stepfather, my stepsisters, my godchildren, my friends, my associates, my business partners, Ms. Morgan, the Bahamas, Broward County, Dade County, Fort Bragg, Sgt. Brothers, SFC Green, SFC Cole, Seth Godin, Robert Kiyosaki, Steve Harvey, Mark Manson, Lenard McKelvey, William Zinsser, Barack Obama, and last but not least, thank you, Lord.

This book is also dedicated to all of my brothers and sisters in the Army, Navy, Marines, Air Force, Coast Guard, National Guard, Reserve, Space Force, Police Department, Sheriff's Department, Highway Patrol, Capitol Police, Campus Police, Fire Department, EMTs, USFWS, USSS, FBI, DEA, US Marshals, DOJ, CBP, ICE, US Park Police, DHS, FLETC, Federal Protective Service, NGA, BIA, Smithsonian Police, DLA, and anyone else who would put their country before themselves.

Finally, this book is dedicated to anyone whose dreams are bigger than the cards they were dealt. To everyone who refuses to let their current state determine their future. To every outside-the-box thinker, to every rags-to-riches success story, to anyone who has the courage to stand for something, to the American dreamer.

CONTENTS

INTRODUCTION

"A young man who does not have what it takes to perform military service is not likely to have what it takes to make a living."

—JOHN F. KENNEDY

If you picked up this book, you're on the right path. A lot of people may ask, "Why should I join the military? All of the dangers, stigmas, negative connotations, are they true? Are the monetary gains enough to compensate for the harsh reality the military brings? Does Uncle Sam really not care about my well-being? Will I end up a disgruntled war veteran?" Fortunately, many of these stigmas are not true. In fact, many of them are complete fallacies. Most are formed due to a lack of exposure to the armed forces or simply just plain old misinformation. The majority of these perceptions derive from a place similar to the rap group Naughty by Nature's song "Other People's Property (OPP)." They stem from other people's opinion (OPO)—what they've heard others say, rather than what they actually know. I believe if people did a little research, they would be pleasantly surprised by the information they find.

Did you know that Reese Witherspoon, Jessica Alba, Tim Kennedy, Steve Carell, C.T. Fletcher, Christina Aguilera, Ciara, Jackie Robinson, Tia and Tamera, Tiger Woods, Michael J. Fox, Pink, Wiz Khalifa, Bruce Willis, Mia Hamm, Elton John, Shaquille O'Neal, Ray Allen, Sean Michaels, Michelle Rodriguez, No Malice, MC Hammer, Ice-T, Nate Dogg, Mystikal, David Goggins, Canibus, Bob Ross, Sharelle Rosado, Morgan Freeman, J. Cole, Mel Brooks, Robert O'Neill, Jimi Hendrix, Drew Carey, Chuck Norris, Elvis Presley, Mr. T, Sean Connery, John Gretton "Jocko" Willink, Montel Williams, Arnold Schwarzenegger, Patrick Bet-David, Sidney Poitier, Clinton Eastwood, Mathew Alfred Best, Bob Barker, Tony Bennett, Johnny Cash, Dulce Candy Ruiz, Willie Nelson, and Harry Belafonte were all either in the military or connected to the military? And that's just to name a few. In fact, the military reaches more affluent people than the average American realizes. The military has influenced leaders of all careers and industries. Many celebrities and people of affluence/authority have close ties to our armed forces. The sad truth is that the average American is clueless to the role the military plays in America's success stories.

FACING THE TRUTH

Let's face it. The average American is in a pickle right now. In fact, you could probably go as far as saying the average American is the pickle in the middle of the poop sandwich, and here's why. Job security is now an American pastime. Inflation was supposed to visit, now it's here to stay. A college graduate takes on average the same number of years they've lived (twenty-one years) to pay off their student loans, the stock market has become more unpredictable than a cat in a room full of dogs, and the American dream (real estate) has been replaced with the American reality (apartments). However, one thing seems to never want to change and that's the American paycheck. Here's the good news in all of this: the solution to many of America's problems is readily available. In fact, it lies within the pages of this book.

Contrary to public opinion, the military is not just a suck-it-up-and-deal-with-the-abuse type of organization. Service members are not trading their freedom for bucks and benefits. The military is way more than that. If you don't believe me, just stick around; the proof will be in the pudding. An individual can gain many positive attributes from serving in our armed forces. Some common traits military service brings are self-discipline, work ethic, integrity, tenacity, punctuality, teamwork, and professionalism. As you may already know, many of these qualities are in short supply to civilians in their day-to-day lives. Values as such could be the difference in what makes someone a success or a failure.

Unfortunately, many Americans have not had the opportunity to see the military for what it actually is. They have ignored the good while putting a highlighter over the bad. There are negative stigmas that have lingered over the armed forces for decades. Stigmas like the military is the last option for most Americans. Or only desperate, extreme left and right people join the military. Or the military destroys families. The truth is the armed forces are a rite of passage for many successful American families. People of all races, classes, and cultures join the military. Everyday people join the military. We all are the military! I strongly believe that the military is an amazing platform that can help an individual get to where they want to be in life. All they have to do is follow the yellow brick road.

Being a former service member, I can say with confidence that the military is not only the place where I gained monetary wealth; it is also where I gained knowledge, experience, discipline, honor, integrity, courage, punctuality, and many other great attributes. The funny thing is that these values not only happen to be core values of the military but are also valued traits within society in general. What I've learned during my transition back to civilian life is that these are in fact life values, a.k.a. keys to success. The truth is, when you come into the military, you come in with what your village or neighborhood instilled in you. But when you leave, you are ingrained with values that are transferable to any industry or environment. These values help you become the best you can possibly be.

I not only believe but I know that there are great benefits to joining the military, and my goal for this book is to bring those benefits to light. To bring into perspective the side of the military people rarely talk about. I am 100 percent certain that every able American should join the military. Not only to gain financial benefits, but to gain mental benefits, character benefits, personal wealth, generational wealth, stability, and prosperity. Traits and benefits that go further than any dollar could. If every able American served our country, I do believe America would be a completely different place. We would have more integrity in our workforce, more honor, more selfless service, more excellence in all that we do, more courage, more commitment, more patriotism, more America. We would literally be all that we could be as Americans. Let's explore this theory a little further.

But first, why should you listen to me? Well, because everything I am preaching I have actually lived. I was born and raised in one of the poorest neighborhoods in the Bahamas. And no, the Bahamas is not just cruise ships and margaritas. My father never finished high school and my mother tried her best as a single mom. In my environment, the wrong decision could have easily landed you in prison or, worse, in the grave. Some of my family members lost their freedom and even their lives to the streets. I came to America with my mother and literally lived life going through the motions. I had no dreams, no ambition, and no concept of success. I went to school because my mother said so. She never had time to ask me what I aspired to be because she was too busy trying to make ends meet. I had no concept of American culture, American history, or the American dream. I was trapped in a prison of mediocrity.

Thankfully, that all changed after I joined the military. It's almost as if the military was my introduction to America. Exposure to America's might, her diverse culture, and possibilities via the military was the wind that helped get my ship sailing. It's almost as if a light bulb switched on. I went from going through the motions to planning my future. From doing things because I was told to do them to doing them because I felt that they were the right things to do. From following my mother to leading my family. From thinking America was one culture to realizing that America is the most diverse nation in the world. From believing that success was set for a chosen few to knowing that success lies in the eye of the beholder.

This shift allowed me to be the first in my family to accomplish many things. I was the first to receive a college degree. The first to own multiple investment properties. The first to manage and maintain a successful stock market portfolio. The first to reach six figures. The first to secure generational wealth. But definitely not the last. This knowledge and experience has been passed down from me to the next generation and beyond within my family. I've watched many of my family members follow the same path and achieve their goals. We've shared our success with one another and all agree that this path needs to reach the masses. Americans young and old need to know the treasure they have lying in their backyard. Too many Americans are suffering in vain. I know this information can help you the way it helped me.

CHAPTER 1

★ ★ ★

WHY I JOINED THE MILITARY

"The only thing we have to fear is fear itself."

—FRANKLIN DELANO ROOSEVELT

I'll never forget the first time I jumped out of a perfectly good airplane. The location was Fort Benning, Georgia. The day was hot and smoggy. Two hundred thirty-six paratroopers in training were crammed into several C-130 aircrafts with one goal in mind, and that goal was to jump out of the plane. I was scared for my life. My heart was pounding but I played it off as though it was just another exercise. In my mind, I had made amends for all of my sins and told God that if today was my last day on Earth, I was ready. The kid to my left was just as scared as me except his face showed it. To my right, another kid had a smirk on his face like he had prepared for that moment his entire life. Standing in the aircraft doorway was the jumpmaster, who had a stone-cold look of confidence on his face. And then it began!

He shouted, "One minute!"

We responded aggressively in unison, "One minute!"

Then he shouted, "Thirty seconds!"

We yelled back, "Thirty seconds!"

The jumpmaster followed by saying, "Outdoor personnel, stand up!"

We shouted back "Outdoor personnel, stand up!"

"Indoor personnel, stand up!"

"Indoor personnel, stand up!" we repeated.

He looked all of us in the eyes and shouted, "Hook up!"

We shouted back, "Hook up!"

He shouted, "Check static line!" and we shouted right back at him, "Check static line."

He shouted, "Check equipment!"

We shouted, "Check equipment!"

Finally, he shouted, "Sound off for equipment check."

One by one we shouted, "Okay!" until the last paratrooper shouted, "All okay, jumpmaster!"

There was an eerie minute or two of silence. The only thing you could hear was the battering sound of the C-130's Allison T56-A engines. Then all of a sudden the jumpmaster yelled, "GO, GO, GO!" And the rest is history. Thirty-six jumps later and all is still okay.

I said all of that to say this: similar to how hurt people hurt people, scared people scare people. You will always have someone telling you don't do that or don't try this. They'll try to scare you out of something. They'll try to put their fears and insecurities on your shoulders to carry.

I've heard so many people say, "Why in the heck would you want to join the military? You're going to die!" Or people who are okay with the military say, "I would join the military but I would never join the Army or the Marines. If you do, you'll go to war and then die." Trust me, from someone who's been there and has done it, do not let other people's fears hinder you from fulfilling your destiny. That destiny may be in the military or it may not be in the military, but whether you join or not, don't base your decision on someone else's fear or manipulation.

HUMBLE BEGINNINGS

I was doing everything that I was supposed to do. Better yet, I was doing everything that was expected of me. I was in college, I had a full-time job, and I was in a stable relationship. Yet something didn't seem right. I was checking all the boxes but still felt like something was missing. I knew where I was, but didn't know what I wanted or where I wanted to be. I was into cars, music, fashion, and spending money on partying. You know, the typical things college-age kids do. Sadly, that wasn't enough. Truth be told, I was trying to find fulfillment in any and everything, but nothing seemed to stick. As Roy Ayers would say, I was "searching, searching, searching." I figured if I pretended to be happy long enough, I eventually would be. Then one day I randomly decided to walk into a recruiter's office and, as they say, "the rest, my friends, is history." Wait, wait, wait, hold on a second...let's rewind a bit.

My random walk into a recruiter's office wasn't as random as I recall. The idea was actually indirectly conceived by my older brother, Dex, a.k.a. Wealth. During his high school years he was in JROTC. He would come home in his uniform, practicing drill and ceremony exercises, which I thought were cool. I remember thinking, *Man, my big brother is so cool; he's strong like Popeye, he knows his drills to the T, and all the ladies love him.* Man, I really wanted to be like my big brother.

But unlike my brother, during high school I was a social introvert. I never cared to socialize with the so-called cool kids. I did play football and received some interest from Wake Forest and Boise State; however, due to my negligence, both schools lost interest. So after high school, I did what my parents wanted me to do and what the majority of young people without a plan do. I went to community college. I was so bored! Bored of my current state, bored of my friends, and bored of my social life. I couldn't see a path out of my mundane existence. I felt like a fish living in the desert. I saw no point in what I was doing at the time.

One day, I decided to look into the military solely out of boredom. I went to the local armed forces recruiting office and spoke to a recruiter. I have to say his demeanor and mannerisms were not what I was expecting. He was cool, calm, and collected, similar to Martin Lawrence's TV show character Bruh Man from the fifth floor. I walked in. He looked up from his chair, nodded, and said, "What's up." I paused for a second as I glanced around the office. He then stood up, his six-foot-three frame towering over me, and said, "How can I help you, young man?" I told him I just wanted some information about the different branches of the military. He pulled up a chair and said, "Have a seat." He broke everything down, all the pros and cons regarding the military. He was frank and honest. He shared the financial and educational benefits, which were great but didn't win me over initially. He told me that if I served a few years, I could gain a lifetime of benefits in return. My recruiter also mentioned to me how joining the military would help me become a better man. So, I went out on a limb and signed up. That decision was one of the best I have ever made. Enlisting in the military changed my life!

IT WORKS!

Not only did being in the military change my life, it changed my family's life as well. It increased my generational wealth and shifted my mentality. I went from your average Joe to financial stability. The decision to join the military secured my family's future and it could do the same for yours. I think about my daughter's future constantly. I wonder if I'm doing enough or if I have done enough to give her a fair chance at success. It's reassuring knowing that her future is secured thanks to the military. The decision to join has given my life a new direction. Direction that I'm now building a legacy on. You could do the same.

During my time in service, I acquired an amazing network of friends and mentors. It included mentors who took me under their wings and stopped me from becoming my own worst enemy. Sergeant Cole, Sergeant Green, and Sergeant Crawford, who were in the middle to latter parts of their careers, showed me the fruits of military labor. They had intentional conversations with me regarding the management of success and failure. They helped me understand not only how to navigate the military but also how to navigate life. Their guidance changed my perspective to not only honor my country but to build on the experience my country provided me. Between Sergeant Cole, Sergeant Green, Sergeant Crawford, my parents, and my family, I've learned how to get the most out of the least. I've learned how to turn off that instant gratification lever in my brain. Equipped with my newfound knowledge, I decided to save my paychecks, work on my financial literacy, and give my life direction. The crazy thing is, I initially joined the military out of pure boredom. But in return I gained discipline, character, integrity, structure, financial literacy, leadership skills, and most importantly stability. It really worked! I now use these skills to thrive in the civilian workspace and also within my own family dynamic. It works! I can't believe it really works!

Okay, enough talking about how great the military is. I'll let the facts speak for themselves. Now, as my old drill instructor Drill Sergeant Street would say, "Let's get down to the meat and potatoes, Hooah."

ONE MORE THING!

Before I finish this chapter, I would like to say this: if you're only joining the military to take advantage of benefits associated with it, I challenge you to dig deeper. Yes, the benefits are great and, trust me, after this book you'll know every single one of them. But if that's the only reason you're joining, I'd rather you not. I challenge you to join for a purpose that's greater than yourself. Join to serve your family, join to serve your community, join to serve your country. As you embark on your journey, also remember to pay your service forward to the next generation. Give someone the chance that you were given. Give them the chance to be great. Great people deserve great things, and every single service member has greatness in them. Remember, less than 1 percent of the 330 million people in America actually join the military, and every single one of them volunteered. Find your place in serving and pay it forward.

CHAPTER 2

★ ★ ★

INCOME LIKE NO OTHER

"Money is numbers and numbers never end. If it takes money to be happy, your search for happiness will never end."

—BOB MARLEY

I remember the first time I saved over ten thousand dollars. I thought I was rich. I felt like Kanye West. I walked around boastfully singing, *"Wait til I get my money right."* If the current me could talk to the old me, he would say, "Man, ten grand, that's nice, but you know that's not a lot of money, right?" The old me probably would have said, "Man, let me be great." Truth be told, I had more in my savings account during my twenties than the average American has in their account during their fifties to sixties. As painful as this statement is, it's sadly true. Saving money has been and continues to be a problem for Americans. Thankfully the military can help ease some of this pain.

Bob Marley was right! Money will never be the answer to happiness; however, if we're being completely honest here, I'm sure we all can agree that it definitely can't hurt. From my experience, you can solve more problems with money than without it. In fact, in America, money takes the bronze medal, only to be beaten by infidelity (silver) and incompatibility (gold) as far as the causes of divorce are concerned. So let's not act like it doesn't matter. With that being said, the military provides income like no other for its service members. Before we get into this chapter, here are some facts regarding the United States commitment to its country's defense. Did you know that the United States defense budget of $1.8 trillion[1] is equivalent to the defense budgets of China, India, United Kingdom, Russia, France, Germany, Saudi Arabia, Japan, and South Korea combined?[2] Crazy, right? Hopefully that gives you a little perspective on America's commitment to its defense. Let's face it, being and staying number one isn't easy, nor is it cheap. The good news for you is that you get a cut of that $1.8 trillion if you're a service member.

THE DIFFERENCE

When I say income like no other, I mean just that. If you were to compare the military base pay (plus food allowance, housing allowance, etc.) to that of the same civilian demographic, you'd notice the difference is staggering. For example, the average seventeen-year-old in Miami, Florida, makes approximately $30,000 ($28,726 exact) per year.[3] However, the average Private 2nd Class (E-2), which would be equivalent to a seventeen- to nineteen-year-old, makes around $62,000 ($62,354 exact) per

---

1   Department of Defense (DOD): FY 2023, USASpending.gov, updated August 30, 2023, https://www.usaspending.gov/agency/department-of-defense?fy=2023.

2   "U.S. Defense Spending Compared to Other Countries," Peter G. Peterson Foundation, April 24, 2023, https://www.pgpf.org/chart-archive/0053_defense-comparison.

3   "Teen Salary in Miami, FL," ZipRecruiter, accessed October 17, 2023, https://www.ziprecruiter.com/Salaries/Teen-Salary-in-Miami,FL#Yearly.

year: $25,790 base pay plus $31,140 basic allowance for housing (BAH) plus $5,424 basic allowance for subsistence (BAS).[4] Note: the BAH in this example is based on an individual with no children. If there were children, the E-2 would receive an additional $10,332 annually. If we were to compare the difference in pay, we would see that the service member makes double what their civilian counterpart makes. That's a $33,628 difference. Bear in mind that this does not include specialty pay, which is a common additional income for service members. Examples of specialty pay are aviation pay ($125 to $1,000 per month), parachute duty pay ($150 to $225), hazardous duty pay ($150), flight deck pay ($150), overseas pay ($300), and many others that I won't waste time going over. If you're curious about the entire list of military additional pay benefits, look them up, but just know the list is long. Bottom line is this: the military pays more and requires less. A $33,000 pay difference is insane when you really think about it. That's like you making $15 an hour and your friend making $32. You both have the same education, same experience, but they make significantly more. That wouldn't make sense to me and I'm sure it doesn't make sense to you. You can bet that the average person in this scenario would probably do one of three things: (1) try to get a job where their friend works, (2) find another job, or (3) find another friend. It's clear that just on basic pay alone, the military outperforms any civilian equivalent by a stretch. I did the math; it's up to you to do the time.

4   "Military Pay 101: Basic Pay, Allowances and S&I Pay," Military OneSource, January 19, 2023, https://www.militaryonesource.mil/military-basics/new-to-the-military/military-pay-101; "2023 Florida BAH (Basic Allowance for Housing) Rates," Veteran.com, updated May 23, 20203, https://veteran.com/bah-rates-state/florida; Jessica Evans, "2023 Basic Allowance for Subsistence (BAS) Rates," The Military Wallet, January 24, 2023, https://themilitarywallet.com/bas-rates.

COMPARE AND CONTRAST

Now here's where it really makes a difference. The pay difference that was calculated did not include expenses. So let's take that same pay difference and calculate some realistic expenses. If you happen to be a nineteen-year-old with a child living on your own, you would more than likely have the following national average monthly expenses: rent $2,011,[5] used car payment $528,[6] food $364[7] per parent plus $155 to $213 child (one year old),[8] day care $1,136,[9] car insurance $265,[10] health insurance $456[11] (parent only; let's assume that the child has government-assisted healthcare). Now, if we calculate these basic deductions, we see that you'd be paying $5,014 in bills before you even got to gas or utilities. Now let's take those bills of $5,014 and deduct them from the parent's monthly income of $2,393 (based on Florida's teens' average annual income of $28,726). That means the parent would be in the hole $2,620 monthly before even paying all of their bills. Sucks, right? Yes, it surely does. That scenario is unfortunately a common one for many Americans. This is why many Americans are forced to get a second job, live with their parents, or apply for gov-

5   Jon Leckie, "The Rent Report: October 2023," Rent.Research, October 16, 2023, https://www.rent.com/research/average-rent-price-report.

6   Shannon Bradley, "What's the Average Car Payment Per Month?," Nerdwallet, updated September 27, 2023, https://www.nerdwallet.com/article/loans/auto-loans/average-monthly-car-payment.

7   Jack Flynn, "Average Cost of Groceries by State [2023]," Zippia, February 27, 2023, https://www.zippia.com/advice/average-cost-of-groceries-by-state.

8   "How Much Does It Cost to Raise a Child?," Western & Southern Financial Group, updated August 31, 2023, https://www.westernsouthern.com/personal-finance/how-much-does-it-cost-to-raise-a-kid.

9   "This Is How Much Child Care Costs in 2023," Care.com, updated July 24, 2023, https://www.care.com/c/how-much-does-child-care-cost.

10   Natalie Todoroff, "Average Cost of Car Insurance in Florida in 2023," Bankrate, updated September 21, 2023, https://www.bankrate.com/insurance/car/average-cost-of-car-insurance-in-florida.

11   Kat Tretina and Heidi Gollub, "How Much Does Health Insurance Cost in 2023?," USA Today, June 23, 2023, https://www.usatoday.com/money/blueprint/health-insurance/how-much-is-health-insurance.

ernment assistance. The good news about this scenario is that the secret to solving it is right in front of you. Unlike the military, civilians normally have to pay for living expenses like housing, food, insurance, etc. Service members, on the other hand, receive allowances in addition to their base pay to cover these expenses. So, not only is the base salary more than that of their civilian counterparts, but military personnel also receive allowances that help mitigate the majority of their expenses. This effect actually increases the extent of their income, making their money stretch further. For example, the same nineteen-year-old parent and child would receive TRICARE free of charge, saving the family hundreds if not thousands of dollars in health expenses, especially if the child does not qualify for Medicaid or has a special medical need. The family would also receive a food allowance for groceries along with military discounts via on-base grocery stores and government assistance programs to help offset their cost. Military housing allowance would cover their rent and could even allow them to purchase a home. If not, free base housing is also available. Last, childcare costs would be heavily discounted via childcare assistance programs that reduce the overall cost of daycare. Regardless of how you look at it, the military completely trumps its civilian counterparts in every way: pay, cost of living, healthcare, and many other monetary factors that have not been accounted for. That's why military income is like no other! Better yet, I'll explain it to you how a service member would: they'd tell you it's the best "bar none."

IT GETS BETTER WITH TIME

The trend of outperforming civil careers only increases as you get older. For example, in the military, on average it takes three to five years to get to the rank of sergeant.[12] If someone enters the military at the age of seventeen, they could be a sergeant, or E-5, by twenty. If we were to keep the demographic the same, the average E-5 salary in Florida is about $78,000 ($77,650 exact): $41,086 (base pay) plus $31,140 (BAH) plus $5,424 (BAS).[13] The average twenty- to twenty-four-year-old civilian makes roughly $37,000 ($37,024 exact).[14] If you noticed, the civilian income on average increased by approximately $7,000 or $3.64 per hour over a three- to five-year period while their military comrade pay increased $16,000 within the same time frame. That $16,000 is equivalent to a $8.30 hourly increase. That's double that of the civilian increase. Now, you tell me which one makes more sense. To sum it up, the military is like fine wine: the longer it sits, the more it's worth.

JOHNNY CASH VS. JOHNNY NO CASH

Johnny Cash decides to join the military at eighteen. At twenty-one he's making over $70,000 a year; his buddy Johnny No Cash is making around $37,000. Johnny No Cash also has accumulated two times the amount of expenses, so he's unable to save. In addition to that he's also taken out several loans just to make ends meet. The two are identical though. They're the same age, neither has a college degree, both are trying to figure

---

12 "Army Promotion to E-5 Sergeant," Military-Ranks.org, accessed October 17, 2023, https://www.military-ranks.org/army/promotion-to-sergeant.

13 Evans, "2023 Basic Allowance for Subsistence (BAS) Rates"; "2023 Florida BAH (Basic Allowance for Housing) Rates," Veteran.com; "Monthly Active Component Basic Pay Table (Effective 1 January 2023)," Defense Finance and Accounting Service, posted January 2023, https://www.dfas.mil/Portals/98/Documents/militarymembers/militarymembers/pay-tables/2023%20AC_RC%20Pay%20Table1.pdf?ver=NUrUfCrNLYPqk6TT20HCXw%3d%3d.

14 "Average Salary in the US by Age and Other Demographics," Capital One, September 4, 2023, https://www.capitalone.com/learn-grow/money-management/what-is-the-average-salary-in-the-us-by-age.

out life, both are contemplating career paths, both love to party and have a good time, and both love music. However, Johnny Cash is crushing it financially; he seems to be doing everything right, while Johnny No Cash is finding it hard to survive. The difference in their outcome is that Johnny Cash decided to join the military and Johnny No Cash never gave it a thought. Due to his financial stability, Johnny Cash decided to get out of the military and pursue his dreams as a musician. He became one of the greatest country artists of all time and eventually helped his buddy Johnny No Cash get out of the rabbit hole.

I KNOW, I KNOW

I know money isn't everything, but I wanted to show you the drastic difference in incomes for two people where the only difference is military service. Again, this is based on basic pay alone. This doesn't include any additional pay or benefits that military personnel receive. Also, for anyone who uses the excuse that money isn't everything to sway people away from their dreams, I have this response for you. You say that money isn't everything because (1) you have money already or (2) you've given up on your pursuit of money. Meaning you've tried and succeeded at obtaining money or you've tried and failed. Either way, you're putting your failure or success on someone else to carry. How about you give them wisdom, knowledge, understanding, and love to carry instead of your success or failure? Tell them the truth: money isn't everything but it definitely matters. If it didn't, we wouldn't get up every weekday to go out and get it. We would stay home, spend time with our families, and do more of the things we love doing instead of getting money if it really didn't matter. Bottom line, money does matter, and with the military you are financially inside the wire or, in other words, financially safe. Without the military you are outside the wire and have to fend for yourself. Which side of the wire are you going to be on?

WHAT'S THE GOAL?

The goal is to compare apples to apples. I want to show you the difference between military careers and civilian careers. The goal is to give you the facts with no fluff and let you decide. I know it worked for me, and it can definitely work for you.

MORE MONEY THAN A RAPPER

For some strange reason everyone wants to be an entertainer nowadays. Whether it's music, sports, Hollywood, or good old social media, everyone wants the money and fame associated with entertainment. I'm sure we've all seen entertainers or commentators brag about how much money this guy or gal got for signing their contracts. Well, if you're into that kind of thing, you're going to enjoy this next section. Another great benefit and difference between a military and civilian career is signing bonuses. People don't realize the amazing signing bonuses that are available via the military. The main difference between civilian careers with signing bonuses and the military is that civilian signing bonuses require education or experience. The military, on the other hand, requires none of the above. You could be a seventeen-year-old kid fresh out of high school, join the military, and get a signing bonus bigger than the advance your favorite rapper got. You could do this with zero education, zero talent, and zero job experience. For example, you can get up to a $50,000 signing bonus if you decide to join the military today (2023), which is absolutely insane. That's literally more than most of today's rappers' initial signing bonuses. Did you know that rap artist Young Thug's first major deal was only worth $30,000? He received $15,000 as a signing bonus and the remaining $15,000 during his contract.[15] Just some food for thought. Let's break down that $50,000 just for perspective. Things you can do with $50,000:

1. Buy a small home
2. Buy land
3. Invest in the stock market
4. Start a business
5. Buy one kilo of gold or seventy kilos of silver
6. Buy many other things that the average eighteen-year-old can't
7. Invest in an e-commerce business
8. Get out of debt

This is a lump sum, by the way, not something that's paid out over time. You get half of the signing bonus when you start basic training and the other half when you finish your individual advanced training. So that's $50,000 at seventeen or eighteen years old, straight into your bank account simply for joining the military and completing training. Signing bonuses can vary depending on a variety of factors such as length of contract, job description, job demand, special skills, foreign language proficiency, etc. For example, a six-year contract in a high-demand military occupational specialty (MOS) has a $50,000 signing bonus. Four years of service in a less demanding field

---

15   Max Weinstein, "Young Thug Reportedly Signed to Atlantic Records for $15K in 2013," Vibe, March 28, 2014, https://www.vibe.com/music/music-news/young-thug-reportedly-signed-atlantic-records-15k-2013-215066.

may offer $20,000. Three years could get you $10,000. It varies widely, and the best way to find out what is available would be to speak to a recruiter. There are also opportunities for additional signing bonuses depending on how high you score, the job you select, how fast you want to be processed through to basic training, and many other factors. Okay, now let's think about this for a second. You could receive tens of thousands of dollars at seventeen to eighteen years old with no experience, no talent, and no education just for joining the military. Where, as a civilian at seventeen or eighteen years old, you would have an extremely difficult time finding a good job that gives you a good paycheck let alone a signing bonus. Like I said, income like no other.

CIVILIAN SIDE OF THINGS

Many civilian signing bonuses require some type of education or experience. The information I am referencing is based on what is currently available in 2023. This could change but I'm certain it will never match the military bonus per education and experience. These examples are straight from indeed.com. Or as young people would say nowadays, this information is brought to you with "no cap."

A radiology technologist (or radiology technician) can get a signing bonus of $2,500. But to qualify you would have to complete a formal radiologic technology program, obtain your state radiologic technologist license, and have a minimum of one year of radiologic technologist experience. Certain trades can get a signing bonus as well, but only after completing the necessary education. An insurance adjuster currently gets up to $10,000, but to qualify you'd need a BA/BS with four to eight years of industry experience. A surgical technician could get a

$20,000 signing bonus but only if they were a licensed practical nurse with a minimum of two years of surgical experience. An electrician could have a $1,500 signing bonus but only after meeting the required two years of residential wiring experience.

Again, all of the civilian jobs that offer signing bonuses offer a fraction of what the military offers and usually require some sort of education or experience. The military signing bonuses can amount to tens of thousands of dollars and require no education or experience other than a high school diploma. Income like no other, my friends, income like no other!

WHAT TO DO WITH YOUR SIGNING BONUS

I would recommend putting your signing bonus into something that can help you grow your wealth (e.g., mutual fund, certificate of deposit, real estate, dividend stocks, exchange traded funds, a personal business, or things of that nature). The point is to not go out and buy a Mustang, pickup truck, old-school American muscle, a girlfriend or boyfriend, jewelry, rims, clothes, motorcycles, or any other depreciating thing an eighteen-year-old would buy. Trust me when I tell you this: invest now and party later. Did you know that approximately 69 percent of Americans have less than $1,000 in their savings account?[16] So, if you were to join the military at eighteen and get a signing bonus, you would automatically have ten to fifty times that of the average American. You can literally place yourself in the top 1 percent in savings within America just by signing up. Seriously! Remember, this does not include additional pay, other bonuses, discounts, and retirement benefits.

---

16 Cameron Huddleston, "Survey: 69% of Americans Have Less than $1,000 in Savings," Yahoo!, December 16, 2019, https://www.yahoo.com/video/survey-69-americans-less-1-171927256.html.

With the military you can literally change your generational wealth. However, it is still up to you to do the right thing with your new influx of cash.

THE SAD TRUTH

Unfortunately, many service members spend their signing bonus as soon as they get it, which puts them back on even footing with their civilian counterparts. As a service member you have to understand the opportunity at hand and take full advantage of it. You have to become financially aware and financially literate. The whole purpose of this book is to bring awareness to Americans about this hidden secret to success. But reading this information alone will not bring you wealth. You have to first realize the opportunity then be disciplined enough to follow through. The information in this book can change your life, but you first have to put that information to work.

CHAPTER 3

★ ★ ★

EDUCATION WITHOUT ATTACHMENTS

"An investment in knowledge pays the best interest."

—BENJAMIN FRANKLIN

Imagine growing up as an average American kid. You're not too tall but not too short, not too fast but not too slow, not too flamboyant but not shy. You have friends but you're not the most popular kid at school. You are the famously known Jack. Yes, the Jack of all, master of none. If you were this guy or gal or knew this guy or gal, then you and I can definitely relate. Growing up, I was your typical all-American kid. I was good at just about everything but had not mastered anything. I was an A/B student, an athlete, a ladies' man, and a frequent principal's honor roll candidate. I even baby-sat the neighborhood kids in my Early Childhood Development class. In fact, I was the first male student to ever take the course at our school. I breezed through elementary, middle school, and high school without even batting an eye. I made it through my scholastic education with no sweat. And then there was college.

When I got to college, I felt as though I was on another plane. The easy breezy education journey stopped with a slap in the face and a cold bucket of reality poured over my head. I felt like a kid who had trained for the Olympics track and field events with sumo wrestlers and now was supposed to compete for the gold medal. I was supposed to represent my Caribbean American culture and make my community proud. I was supposed to take everything I had learned and apply it. Yeah, that was the problem: I hadn't learned much. Upon my arrival to college I realized that my education was not Principal's Honor Roll, it was more like Janitor's Honor Roll. I realized that even though I was one of the better students at my school, I had not been equipped with enough knowledge to even compete, let alone be successful. I failed basic college math and was placed in an intermediate math course. I also discovered that I did not know how to read, which landed me in an ESOL class. ESOL, if you don't know, spells out the acronym English for Speakers of Other Languages. Everyone in the class spoke another language but me. I was educationally shell-shocked. I couldn't believe that my life's worth of education amounted to intermediate math and an ESOL class.

That experience hurt me so much that I kept it from my family for years. I remember talking to my mother about my experience some years later and her saying, "Son, I am so sorry that you were robbed of an education. However, don't be discouraged, because once you have one, no one can ever rob you of it again." I took those words and carried them from my community college to my community university and from my community university to the University of Miami, where I eventually received my master's degree. Benjamin Franklin knew in the 1700s what many still have not realized today: knowledge is the best investment you can ever make for yourself. A fisherman doesn't need a supermarket. Learn and you'll never have to ask.

IT'S IMPORTANT

I think it's important for people to know what they are missing out on by not joining the military. For example, with the GI Bill, I was able to attend college and not only have my tuition completely paid for, but I was also paid a salary while I was in school. That was approximately $300,000 worth of education, by the way. I was able to attain my associate's, my bachelor's, and my master's degree for zero dollars and zero cents thanks to the military.

Furthermore, people think the GI Bill only covers traditional schooling. However, you can also get certifications and licenses, go to flight school or vocational school, be reimbursed for national testing programs, and much more. Not only is your school paid for, but you will get paid to be educated!

For example, when I got my master's degree at the University of Miami, the cost was roughly $220,000. I paid *zero dollars*. And the military also paid me approximately $2,400 per month to go to school. So not only was I getting a free ride, I was putting $28,800 in my pocket every year. Seems as though service members were getting NIL (name, image, and likeness) money before it existed. The allowance is based on your particular state's cost of living. So in my example, Florida's cost of living was $2,400; that's $115,200 over the course of four years just for pursuing an education. like I said, NIL money!

Let's say someone goes into the military at eighteen and gets out when they're twenty-two. If they're smart they would go back to their parents' house, live there, and go to school using the GI Bill. The GI Bill covers tuition and pays essentially the equivalent of a full-time salary gig while the person is in school. If they are able to keep their living expenses low, they could save their allowance money and come out of college with a degree, debt-free, and with six figures in their savings account.

That's what I want people to see: the value they're getting. And that's just the beginning of the value when it comes to the education benefits. Not only do they pay for your basic housing allowance, you also get money for books and tools needed for your education. So every three to six months you get an additional amount of income on top of your housing allowance.

There's also the GI Plus, which allows a veteran to include their children or spouse. I don't know about you, but I haven't heard of any other organization that offers such benefits.

WHAT AN EDUCATION CAN DO FOR YOU

Education isn't everything, but it is a lot. If you're looking at a corporate job, most want a four-year degree, minimum. So if you don't have a four-year degree you automatically disqualify yourself from those jobs. You wouldn't want to be denied employment just for not having a piece of paper. And the fact that the military is giving you the means to an end speaks volumes. There is also a big difference in the salary and success of people who have a four-year degree versus those who don't. In fact, bachelor's degree holders make $36,000 more annually than those who only possess a high school diploma.[17] That's equivalent to $1.2 million more over their lifetime.

Here's what it would cost you if you didn't have military benefits. According to EducationData.org, the average cost of

---

17 "How Does a College Degree Improve Graduates' Employment and Earnings Potential?," Association of Public & Land-Grant Universities, accessed October 17, 2023, https://www.aplu.org/our-work/4-policy-and-advocacy/publicuvalues/employment-earnings.

tuition for a four-year institution is $28,775, which is $9,349 per year.[18] So if you were to pay for your own education, you would have to come up with almost $30,000. And while $9,349 per year seems reasonable, it doesn't include cost of living: housing, food, transportation, books, and supplies. This is where the military really comes out ahead. As a civilian, a twenty-two-year-old has to find a way to pay $30,000 for tuition plus living expenses. This will more than likely lead them down the path to a student loan. And not only will they need to borrow money to cover tuition, they will likely need money to cover living expenses. This is a heavy load to put on a twenty-two-year-old and could impact their chance of completing the degree, which will ultimately impact their employment opportunities.

The military also offers benefits to help your family succeed. If you're a family-oriented person, or even if you're not thinking that way because you're only twenty-two, you should seriously consider paying the extra fee for GI Plus. GI Plus allows your kids' education to be paid for under your GI Bill. This contributes to generational wealth by giving the next generation better opportunities and chances to succeed. It's such a simple thing, but it makes a huge difference.

Some may say dealing with the hardships of their financial burdens is still preferable to the possible hardships from being in the military. They do not want their freedom restricted or are concerned about going to war. They'd rather deal with their reality than to risk it. However, numbers don't lie. Did you know that 30 to 40 percent of all service jobs are combat-related? Furthermore, only 10 to 20 percent of all service members ever

---

18   Melanie Hanson, "Average Cost of College & Tuition," Education Data Initiative, updated September 6, 2023, https://educationdata.org/average-cost-of-college.

see combat.[19] So trust me, it's not as bad as they make it out to be. Here's some personal experience to give you a little more perspective about how amazing the military education benefits are. I vividly remember meeting an attorney at a social gathering. A white woman in her early thirties, she was complaining about her student loans. Now remember, she's an attorney. She made good money, but she said because of her student loans she wasn't able to afford a house. On the outside she looked successful—good clothes, nice car, nice apartment—but she didn't have any true wealth. Her student debt was consuming her. I asked her later how much student debt she had and she said $200,000 plus interest. I'm assuming it will probably take her at least ten years to pay that off. Imagine that: drowning in $200,000 worth of debt that you have to pay just to give yourself a better life. It's examples like this that assure me that the military just makes sense.

Even if you're not using your GI Bill to go to law school, you have a greater chance of success and generational wealth because you will come out of school debt-free. For me in particular, by the time I graduated from college I already had a property that had generated equity. But this attorney who had paid for her own education now couldn't afford a home. So even if her income was higher than mine, I had more wealth.

I know it might look like a sacrifice, especially in times of war; however, in life sometimes you have to face challenges like a marathon runner. You can't see the finish line to motivate your effort; nonetheless, you know a finish line exists. These benefits are lifetime benefits that will change your future. That's what I want young men and women to understand. It's bigger than

---

19   "What Percentage of Soldiers See Combat?," Midwest Disability, December 13, 2019, https://www. midwestdisability.com/blog/2019/12/what-percentage-of-soldiers-see-combat.

the paycheck that you get from the military. It's even bigger than the fact that you get an education for free. These things can affect you for years. For example, let's say you get a student loan to go to school and it takes fifteen years to pay it back. If you simply did three to five years in the military, that money you invested in that student loan could have been going toward developing family or generational wealth.

I just want people to see all the benefits that are already there. It's crazy because people don't look at the intricate details of the perks they're getting. For example, my nephew is in the military and was thinking about leaving when I told him that without the GI Bill alone, he could possibly be throwing away a couple hundred thousand dollars in covered education costs and salary. But it's more than that. There are also all the incalculable benefits of that education. My nephew doesn't know where that education might take him. Same for you. You may go to a four-year college and meet a group of people that change your network, change your circle, and change your life.

I want our young people to see that the simple act of joining the military could change their entire life. I didn't recognize the benefits of joining the military until I got out. What job in America offers these benefits? None. Even if you have a job that offers tuition assistance, it's usually only a couple of bucks and there's always some string attached like requiring a degree in a certain field or requiring you to work for that company for a certain amount of time.

Compare and contrast for yourself, but it's Johnny Cash versus Johnny No Cash. Think about it. You could pay for it yourself and become like the attorney I met at the party who looked wealthy but was drowning in debt. Or, you can start building generational wealth and networking with the best of the best, all for free.

CHAPTER 4

★ ★ ★

TRAVEL THE WORLD ON A DIME

"There is nothing like returning to a place that remains unchanged to find the ways in which you yourself have altered."

—NELSON MANDELA

I remember my first experience with the US military on foreign soil. It was interesting to say the least. I was in the Bahamas visiting my grandmother on one of the remote islands where the population is so small the residents could probably all fit in a Walmart parking lot. We were driving on the main road of the island when I started noticing a ton of what looked like Special Forces body types randomly jogging down the street. I was puzzled. I didn't understand why there were so many military personnel running down the main road of the island. I thought to myself, *Maybe it's some type of marathon or maybe Groupon was giving out some really great discounts to joggers who want to visit the Bahamas.* Heck, I didn't know. So I asked my uncle. He said, "Oh, those are just the US troops doing their morning workout."

"Wait, what?!" US troops? My mind was blown.

"Yup, there is a military base on the island but it's kind of hidden. You would only know it if you lived here or were stationed on base."

I was stunned. I couldn't believe I paid to visit my grandmother when I could have hitched a ride on a C-130!

Have you ever traveled to an exotic destination like Africa, Europe, Asia, or the Caribbean and just happened to notice US troops in uniform? Believe it or not, those troops you saw were more than likely on duty. Yes, that's correct; they're working and living in the places you paid to visit. Oh, and I forgot to mention, they're working and living there at no cost to them. "Traveling on a dime" or traveling at little to no expense is another amazing benefit of being a service member.

The military is one of those careers that afford service members the opportunity to travel the world practically for free. Whether you're stationed overseas or traveling for training, the military provides many opportunities for service members to travel domestically and internationally. And you're often traveling to places you would have likely never visited on your own.

DO YOU KNOW?

Were you aware that there are over 750 US military bases in over eighty countries and territories around the globe?[20] Crazy, right? That's what I thought when I first read those statistics. If you decided to join the military, you could end up in Germany, Japan, South Korea, Italy, Bahamas, Bahrain, Virgin Islands, Kenya, Cuba, Spain, Turkey, Tunisia, UK, Jordan, Ireland, Oman, Philippines, Qatar, Wake Island, Honduras, Norway, Kuwait,

20   Tyler McBrien, "Why the U.S. Should Close Its Overseas Military Bases," Foreign Policy, May 16, 2023, https://foreignpolicy.com/2023/05/16/military-defense-overseas-bases-united-states-force-posture.

Kosovo, Peru, Israel, Saudi Arabia, Canada, Australia, and many other amazing places around the globe. Oh, and don't forget about the locations the military is not allowed to disclose. You could end up there too. So truthfully, you could end up visiting or living just about anywhere on planet Earth via the military. Now tell me what other occupation would do that for a seventeen-year-old kid fresh out of high school. As rap artist Biggie Smalls would say, *If you don't know, now you know.*

I've been fortunate to visit quite a few places during my time in service. While training, I traveled to Georgia, North Carolina, South Carolina, DC, and Maryland. Places I would not have traveled to on my own. And get this: it was all free. The experience I gained from these trips is incomparable. I started out with the perspective of a typical Caribbean kid, who had never ventured much beyond my neighborhood, and ended up being exposed to so much more.

I also went to Germany as part of my career. I met some amazing people there. That experience alone changed my outlook of Europe, the US, and life in general. I remember the culture, the food, the people. It was like watching a foreign movie starring yourself. The locals saying *"Guten morgen,"* calculating dollars to euros, traveling on the Autobahn: these were all things I had never experienced before. And if I had not joined the military, I would not have the perspective I have today.

Traveling the world on a dime is about more than traveling the globe for free. It's not just about the cool locations, it's about gaining perspective. It's about the experience. Whether it's realizing how blessed you are or realizing how big the world is, traveling changes you. Traveling can be refreshing and it can also be sobering. It's an opportunity to gain exposure to other cultures in a way you wouldn't otherwise, whether it's a completely different culture or a subculture within your own.

There's a sense of enlightenment that comes with travel, and fortunately for service members it's a part of the job.

A great example of how traveling via the military is beneficial can be seen through the experience of a colleague of mine. He was stationed in Asia during a portion of his career. His exposure to Asian culture changed his life. It influenced his personality, his demeanor, and ultimately his perspective. He loved his time in Asia so much that he decided to live there after he completed his enlistment. He got out, got married, and built a new life in Asia for himself. If he wasn't in the military, more than likely, he wouldn't have traveled to Asia (he's a country kid who may have never had the money or opportunity to travel there on his own) and never would have had the life he has today.

DON'T BECOME A HOSTAGE TO YOUR ENVIRONMENT

During my military career, I traveled to Florida; Georgia; North Carolina; South Carolina; Texas; Maine; Washington, DC; Maryland; Afghanistan; Kuwait; Kyrgyzstan; and Germany. Of the places I've visited, there were three that had the greatest influence on me: Afghanistan, Germany, and Maryland. Afghanistan was very sobering. It made me appreciate the abundance we have in America. The poverty was heartbreaking. Just seeing the state of the people, the impact of war, and the unthinkable living conditions made me appreciate how blessed we are as Americans, especially in terms of having the freedom and opportunity to make our own decisions. Sadly, the people of Afghanistan and many other places around the globe are held hostage by their environment due to economic or political oppression. The young Afghan men I encountered were mostly uneducated, with little motivation to become educated. They had limited opportunities. That's why the Taliban and Al-Qaeda were able to infiltrate many villages so easily. They manipulated young people who had no hope of escaping their environment to plant bombs or fight US troops for money.

Seeing how many options we have in America compared to people in other countries made me grateful. Even something as simple as deciding where and what to eat on a daily basis. I can wake up and decide I want to eat at McDonald's today. Or, if I don't like the job I have, I can go get another one, a better one! Or I can decide to go to college. People in other countries don't have those types of choices. Not being held hostage by our environment is something we truly take for granted here in America. Even something as basic as our air quality. I say this next statement with all love and respect for decent, hardworking Afghans. If you've ever been to Afghanistan, the first thing you notice is how bad the air quality is. I noticed it as soon as I got off the plane: Afghanistan smells like poop. Why? Because people burn their own excrement in order to dispose of it. And if it isn't burned, it's dumped in a giant hole and left to sit there. Something as simple as our utilities or sewage system is another luxury most Americans take for granted. Thank God we don't have to burn or dump our poop to dispose of it.

BEAUTY THAT INSPIRED

Germany also made an impact on me due to how beautiful and patriotic the country is. I was in Germany for about a month. I was in Frankfurt for the most part, and I remember it being a very upbeat, happy, vibrant town. I would go into a bar and be greeted with a smile. The hospitality is definitely something I'll never forget. The people there were so unified, I was envious. It made me wish that Americans were more in sync with one another. In America, there are so many different cultures and subcultures it's easy to become divided. There are multiple cultures in Germany too, but there was a great sense of unity, a high level of patriotism, and a love of being German that was easily identifiable.

In Germany, most people spoke English as a second language. I remember riding the bus and being asked if I was American. I asked the individual why they assumed that and they stated it was because Americans only speak one language. Funny enough, I was on vacation in the Dominican Republic and a native said something similar, that most Americans can only speak English.

When I came back from Germany, I was motivated to connect with people outside of my culture. To try and understand people of different mindsets, beliefs, religions, and cultures. It made me want to connect with people who say they are patriotic but do not associate with other Americans who are different from them. Honestly, that's something I struggle to understand. How can you hate someone who's rooting for the same team? It doesn't make sense. You both want the home team to win, right? Of course you do. So why can't you accept them as they are if they want the same thing you want? I digress. As I was saying, I wanted to connect with my countrymen and women in a way I had never wanted to before. I realized there was a better way of living as one, and I got that from Germany.

COLD SHOULDER

Maryland, on the other hand, was the complete opposite. It was a huge culture shock for me. It's only about a fifteen-hour drive from where I grew up but it felt like another planet. I was in Maryland for about two to three months. I remember it having a "Rocky Balboa" feel. It was very scrappy, very much an every-man-for-himself mentality, and a look-over-your-shoulder culture. Full disclosure, the area I'm describing is not the entire state of Maryland. So before you start, let me stop you. Maryland the state is probably great, but where I ended up wasn't. I grew up in the South, and when I would approach people in Maryland with my Southern hospitality I'd be greeted with hostility. I remember everyone being guarded, which I didn't understand at the time. It was a tense environment, not only on the military side, but with civilians as well. It was really dark, gloomy, and cold. The sun only came out a few times while I was there. I guess it felt unwelcome too.

The way young people in Maryland dressed, the colors they wore, and their overall demeanor were way more aggressive than what I was used to growing up in Florida. And let's not forget how hood or country Florida can get. The Sunshine State is definitely nothing to play with. However, in Florida, we wear bright summer colors and are laid back (for the most part). We give the energy we receive, if you know what I mean. In Maryland the demeanor was guarded and standoffish. Even though Florida and Maryland are geographically close, they are completely different in culture. Being stationed there made me appreciate the southern hospitality we have in Florida. And truthfully, I felt more at home in Germany than I did in Maryland, which is sad. But I'll leave that conversation for another day.

As for South Carolina, I remember it being very country. I got a little bit of everything there: a bit of southern hospitality and a bit of hostility. It was a very balanced state. I felt like I was more of a spectator during my time in North and South Carolina. I would stand back and observe the clashes of personality, the clashes of culture, and the clashes of good, bad, and everything in between.

BUT HERE'S WHAT'S IMPORTANT

These are experiences I would have never had outside of the military. Not just the traveling itself, but the memories and the perspective. Sure, some of the places I've been to I could have traveled to on my own, but some I couldn't. And even with the places I would have been able to travel to myself—Maryland, for example—traveling there as part of the military gave me an opportunity to see a different way of living. If I had traveled to Maryland on my own, I may have seen some sights and had a good time, but I wouldn't have been able to experience the culture and people the way I did traveling there as part of the military. In the military, I was there to train and was able to spend much more time than I would have on my own. This allowed me to get to know the people and the culture.

Every place I've been to has given me a new perspective of myself and the world. I was in Afghanistan for fifteen months. It was originally supposed to be twelve months, but my unit got "stop-lost" due to our replacement not being ready. The biggest memory I have of Afghanistan is my interaction with the local Afghan kids. There are kids *everywhere*. Every village you go to, there are at least twenty kids running around outside. This stuck out to me because they all looked like they had nowhere to go and had no direction. Kids in the United States are always on the move because they have somewhere to be—they're headed to school, or from school, or to friends or activities. In Afghanistan, the kids are just playing outside with seemingly nowhere else to go. And when we would go into a village, the kids would run up to us and tug on our uniforms asking for candy and chocolate. That candy and chocolate was the world to them. For us it's just a Snickers bar, a Starburst, but for them it brought so much joy.

I also remember the oppression of women. They were

muted and many wore burqas. It was almost as if they didn't exist. If they came out while we were there, they would quickly hide themselves. It was very sobering to see how far America has come with the liberation of women in comparison to some other parts of the world. I remember talking to a couple of women who were blessed enough to attend college. They said that if it weren't for their father or family member being in a certain political position, they could be beaten or killed simply for going to school or exposing their faces.

Traveling is one of the most undervalued perks of being in the military. What other job, especially one you can qualify for at seventeen with no education or training experience, would allow you to travel the world, *as part of your job*? I can't think of any. And if there were any, they would likely require a high level of education or skill.

CHAPTER 5

★ ★ ★

GENERATIONAL CHANGE

"A good man leaves an inheritance to his children's children, but the sinner's wealth is laid up for the righteous."

—PROVERBS 13:22

When most people think of the Bahamas, they immediately think of sand, beautiful beaches, swimming pigs, margaritas, and cruise ships. In fact, Swisspath Yachting calls it "paradise on earth"[21] and *The Bahamas Investor* calls it "the playground for the uber rich."[22] That's most people's view of the Bahamas. However, my experience growing up was slightly different and I say that sarcastically. What many tourists and multimillionaires don't know is that approximately 12 percent of the population's annual income is less than $5,000.[23] That's $416 a month, $104

---

21 "The Breathtaking Bahamas, Paradise on Earth," Swisspath Yachting, September 25, 2020, https://www. swisspath-yachting.com/the-breathtaking-bahamas.

22 Gillian Beckett, "The Bahamas—Playground for the Uber Rich," The Bahamas Investor Magazine, January 1, 2009, https://www.thebahamasinvestor.com/2009/ the-bahamas-playground-for-the-uber-rich.

23 Anthony Pratt, "Poverty in the Bahamas," editorial, Tribune (Nassau, The Bahamas), October 15, 2019, http://www.tribune242.com/news/2019/oct/16/poverty-bahamas.

per week, or $2.60 an hour. Now imagine trying to feed a family on $2.60 an hour. I remember nights waiting for my parents to bring something home to eat. I remember having to use candles when the lights went out, and they went out frequently. Abandoned cars that have been parked in the same spot for so long that trees and wildlife have inhabited them. Drug addicts and homeless people walking the streets like zombies. Sleeping in your bed knowing that a roach, mosquito, or mouse would more than likely cross paths with you at night. Even though it's only 12 percent of the population, to those 12 percent it feels like they are living Palaye Royale's "Nightmare in Paradise" 100 percent of the time.

I mention my childhood of poverty in the Bahamas because this same story has been told millions of times, for hundreds of years. The story of generational poverty is nothing new. Just change the names and locations of the people and it's literally the same story. To paraphrase Digital Underground and Jay-Z, all around, it's the same song. Generational wealth or poverty begins as an inherited financial status but ultimately manifests itself into a state of mind. Generational wealth is never guaranteed. In fact, 70 percent of families lose their generational wealth by the second generation, and 90 percent will lose it by the third generation.[24] This normally occurs due to the lack of conversation and transparency regarding family wealth and a lack of financial literacy when it comes to asset management.

Now that you have the rundown on generational poverty and wealth, let's take a look at why the military has the potential to create generational wealth.

---

24 Chris Taylor, "70% of Rich Families Lose Their Wealth by the Second Generation," Money, June 17, 2015, https://money.com/rich-families-lose-wealth.

GET-RICH-QUICK GENERATION

In a modern world of get-rich-quick phrases and antics, it can be difficult knowing whether a particular thing can change your generational wealth. Let's face it, this generation is the get-rich-quick generation. Everyone wants to get rich off their part-time gig. How many times this week have you seen an ad or heard someone say, "This (fill in the blank) side hustle, investment, or financial strategy can make you super rich in no time. Just follow these (fill in the blank amount of) steps and sign up for my so-called free course"? If it's so easy to get rich, why is the majority of the world poor? I'll let you answer that part.

Goal of this chapter: to get you rich. No, no, I'm only kidding. This is not a get-rich-quick book. This is a "get educated, get benefits, get character, and eventually gain wealth" book. The factors discussed in this chapter can bring generational wealth. This means taking advantage of the benefits in front of you, which can change your status in a positive way. MC Hammer is the perfect example of how the military can change your generational wealth. The net worth of Stanley Kirk Burrell, a.k.a. MC Hammer, reached $70 million in the nineties.[25] To give you a little perspective, that is equivalent to $164 million in today's economy. MC Hammer grew up in Oakland, California, surrounded by drugs, gangs, and poverty. Generational wealth was probably the last thing on his mind. But Hammer did what many children in his neighborhood didn't. He joined the military. The benefits from his three-year naval service gave him enough stability to pursue his career in music. He went from poverty to multimillionaire after serving in the armed forces,

---

25   Jacob Uitti, "MC Hammer's Net Worth: From 'U Can't Touch This' to 'The Addams Family'," American Songwriter, October, 2022, https://americansongwriter.com/mc-hammers-net-worth-from-u-cant-touch-this-to-the-addams-family/.

and don't think this was a coincidence. Sadly for Hammer, the lack of financial literacy caused him to lose that wealth.

THINGS THE MILITARY GIVES YOU THAT COULD CHANGE YOUR GENERATION
HOUSING

The VA loan is one of the biggest financial benefits the military offers. With a VA loan, veterans can gain wealth by purchasing real estate. Why is real estate such a big factor in generational wealth? First thing is everyone needs somewhere to live. You can either live on someone's property or live on your own property. If you purchase real estate, you are now able to take the funds used to pay for shelter and invest them into yourself. You can pay down your mortgage while gaining net worth from your assets. Also, if you continue to live or possess that property, you'll have a tangible asset to hand over to the next generation. Plus, unlike traditional buyers, you are not required to put 20 percent down to secure a loan. Nor do you have to pay mortgage insurance. Taking advantage of this could change your financial trajectory. You could go from renter to landlord. Your home can be paid off and passed on to the next generation.

EDUCATION

I'll be short with this because I already explained this benefit in Chapter 3. There are few possessions like education. Education may not be something you can touch, feel, or visit during the summers, but it is an asset no one can take away from you. It can be a blessing and open up doors that were previously closed or it can become a burden of truth. It is up to you what you decide to do with it. Thankfully, service members are able to experience this journey at no cost. I'll leave you with this: education is similar to a rack of clothes at your favorite boutique. The choice is yours to make. You just have to be comfortable with the cost associated with the choice. Education as a veteran is your choice to make as well; the only difference is there is no cost associated with your decision.

INTANGIBLES

The military equips you with a number of intangibles that are hard to come by otherwise.

Leadership

When you join the military you are taught to not only embrace the role of leadership but to perfect it. This skill is definitely overlooked. Many service members find the stress associated with leadership in a civilian career easy compared to the stresses of leadership via the military. This tends to give service members an advantage over their civilian counterparts. I remember being in charge of millions of dollars in military equipment and responsible for the well-being of hundreds of service members on the biggest airfield in Afghanistan—and I was not even the tip of the sword. No wonder service members are not fazed by leadership roles in the private sector. These traits are also transferable to service members' future generations. As Proverbs 22:6 says, "Train up a child in the way he should go; even when he is old he will not depart from it."

Punctuality

All service members know if you're early, you're on time; if you're on time, you're late; if you're late, you're done. Punctuality is not a bonus; it's a requirement. It shows your commitment to your cause. This concept is continually reinforced in the military and is a key factor to success.

Teamwork

Teamwork is not essential in every career field. However, it can take a bad situation and make it good, take a good situation and make it great, take a great situation and make it amazing. Many Americans never learned how to swim due to the fear of water. Similarly, many citizens never practice working in a team setting because it's not required, ultimately never learning how to function in the environment. Here is my advice: don't wait until you need to swim to learn how to swim.

Integrity

Integrity is by far the greatest intangible an individual gains during their time in service. Integrity is doing the right thing even when it feels like it's the wrong time. Integrity is the shield that covers the heart of a service member's character. Integrity equals honor; honor equals service; service equals purpose; purpose equals destiny. Without integrity, the military would implode, just as we've seen with so many unfortunate corporations.

Courage

Courage is the ability to do something that frightens you. Let's face it, we all could use a little courage in our day-to-day lives. You step up to take charge of the meeting at work. You overcome your fear or phobia. You face a problem head-on. All of these actions take courage.

These values can change your generation. Again, these things are not a get-rich-quick scheme. These are great stepping stones, stepping stones that will help elevate your life. Remember, just because you're changing your generational wealth does not mean you're going to be a millionaire. Money isn't everything. It's about the quality of life.

I've personally had several relatives experience this shift via the military. Before their military experience, they went through life guided by nothing more than self-gratification. But instead of staying on that path and possibly becoming a statistic, they are now successful citizens. Thanks to the military, they have financial stability, their children can go to school for free, and they have a good quality of life. This is what it's all about.

CHAPTER 6

★ ★ ★

BEST HEALTHCARE IN AMERICA

"Our health is the most important thing we have."

—CRISTIANO RONALDO

I'll never forget the day I realized human beings are not invincible. It was summertime in Florida. I was living a normal life, with a normal family, in a normal neighborhood. I had gotten so comfortable with normalcy that I fell into a routine. That routine was work, home, church. Hours turned into days, days turned into months, and months turned into years. I remember thinking to myself, *Man, time flies.* Watching my life was like watching a clock on the wall in time-lapse mode. Then my mother called. My mom (or as we would say in Bahamian, "my momi") FaceTimed me and told me that I needed to come to the hospital. In an instant, my heart dropped. I knew no one had died because my mother wears her emotions on her sleeve and she wasn't crying, but I also knew it wasn't good because she told me to come now.

I said, "Momi, are you okay, is everything all right?"

She said, "Yeah, baby, I'm okay. It's not me; it's Dex."

For some reason I was relieved. I thought to myself, *Oh, Dex is in the hospital, okay.* I was relieved because I knew if it was serious, my mother's shoulders would have figuratively told me. She wasn't crying and didn't seem distraught so I figured it wasn't anything major. Plus, my big brother Dex was the Popeye of the family. He was the pretty boy with the model body. I figured it was probably just a bad cold or something. Also, my mother was big on family supporting each other so she probably just wanted us to be there for support. I took a shower, threw on some clothes, and headed to the hospital, which was about forty-five minutes away. On the way, I stopped and picked up a balloon and flowers from the local convenience store, hoping it would bring him a little joy.

When I got there, Dex was sitting up in the bed with a hospital robe on. I thought to myself, *Oh boy, he is wearing a hospital robe. That either means he's been here for a while or is going to be here for a while.* I greeted him in our Bahamian patois: "Dex, what you saying? Everything cool?"

He replied, "Everything cool, li'l bro."

I tried to make light of the situation by cracking a few jokes. He laughed but you could tell he was concerned about the hospital visit. Then my mother filled me in: according to the doctors, Dex had an unusual amount of fluid buildup around his heart and lungs, which caused a shortness of breath. They were not sure what brought on the excess fluid but were leaning toward lupus. My mother, with her spiritual background, rebuked the notion. Eventually they got the fluid out of Dex and he was released from the hospital. Who would have known that night was the beginning of a journey that would change not only my brother's life but my family's life as well? Fifty hospital visits, fifteen major surgeries, and millions of dollars in health costs later, I look back and think to myself, *That was the day I realized Superman was not invincible.* Life is short, health is fragile, and healthcare is expensive. Thank God my brother's wife had good health insurance. If she didn't, who knows where my brother's health would be today. Sadly, many American families go through this exact scenario but don't make it out on top. They are either consumed by the cost of major surgery or succumb to their illness.

WORDS FROM THE WISE

Cristiano Ronaldo is one of the richest athletes in the world. He has made a good living off of his natural abilities. Not only is he worth half a billion dollars, he's also the most popular human being on the planet, according to social media. One of his most famous quotes is "Our health is the most important thing we have."[26] If someone worth a half billion dollars—not to mention, someone with a half billion followers—says our health is the most important thing we have, I'll take their word on it. I mean, Mr. Ronaldo can literally have anything he wants but he chooses his health. That says a lot! In fact, it reminds me of when NBA superstar LeBron James took his talents to South Beach. LeBron was dominant in Cleveland but he became legendary when he started taking his health seriously in Miami. The results were evident off the court as well.

---

26   Cristiano Ronaldo (@Cristiano), "Our health is the most important thing we have. How are you practicing good #fitness and #nutrition habits? @Herbalife Nutrition," Twitter, May 16, 2020, https://twitter.com/Cristiano/status/1261705619456831489?lang=en.

THE SAD TRUTH ABOUT AMERICA

The United States is an extremely competitive country. Regardless of the topic or category, Lady Liberty always finds a way to end up on top. In fact, create a new competition and watch Lady Liberty attempt to conquer it. The same sentiment, however, cannot be applied when discussing Lady Liberty's health. Were you aware that the United States ranks dead last in overall health care when compared to other industrialized countries? The key elements of the ranking include overall population health, access to healthcare, efficiency of healthcare, equity of healthcare, and overall quality of healthcare.[27] I know this news is just as shocking to you as it was to me; however, that's not all. I hate being the guy to make bad news worse, but not only does Lady Liberty have the worst healthcare, she also has the most expensive healthcare. So not only are Americans getting the worst healthcare available in an industrialized nation, they're also paying the most for it. That double whammy is definitely sobering. Here are the rankings:

1. United Kingdom
2. Switzerland
3. Sweden
4. Australia
5. Netherlands
6. New Zealand
7. Norway
8. France
9. Canada
10. United States

---

27 "U.S. Ranks Last Among Seven Countries on Health System Performance Measures," newsletter article, The Commonwealth Fund, accessed October 17, 2023, https://www.commonwealthfund.org/publications/newsletter-article/us-ranks-last-among-seven-countries-health-system-performance.

WHAT'S KILLING AMERICANS

If you ask the average American on the street what they think the leading cause of death in America is, most would probably say homicide. Well, they would definitely be on target, it just wouldn't be a bull's-eye. According to the CDC, the leading cause of death for young Americans (ages one to forty-four) has been, and more than likely will continue to be, unintentional injuries.[28] This includes opioid overdoses, motor vehicle crashes, and unintentional falls. The second and third leading causes of death are suicide (which could probably be reduced in a better mental healthcare system) and homicide (which is a whole other book in itself). The other seven leading causes of death are all preventable, or at a minimum reducible, with the right healthcare. Those remaining causes are heart disease, malignant cancer, COVID-19, liver disease, diabetes, stroke, and influenza/pneumonia. The bottom line is that we have to do better as a nation with healthcare, no excuses. We generate way too much revenue to have a healthcare system this bad.

WHAT DOES THE MILITARY HAVE TO DO WITH IT?

I know that intro was a lot, and most of you probably speed-read through it. But it was necessary for the topic at hand. Why does the military have the best healthcare in America? Well, the first reason is the cost. The average American spends eight to thirteen thousand dollars annually for healthcare.[29] Just to give you a little perspective, you would have to work a full-time job

---

28 "Top Ten Leading Causes of Death in the U.S. for Ages 1–44 from 1981–2020," Centers for Disease Control and Prevention, reviewed February 28, 2023, https://www.cdc.gov/injury/wisqars/animated-leading-causes.html.

29 "Why Are Americans Paying More for Healthcare?," Peter G. Peterson Foundation, July 14, 2023, https://www.pgpf.org/blog/2023/07/why-are-americans-paying-more-for-healthcare.

making eight dollars an hour for a year to pay that bill. Thank God for credit cards! Without America's loaning system, most Americans would not be able to afford such a bill.

Now let's compare these numbers to the cost of healthcare for service members. After years of research and hours upon hours of statistical data collection, we are proud to announce the true cost of healthcare for service members. As of 2023 the true cost of healthcare for service members is zero dollars. Through systems like TRICARE and the VA service, members can pay zero (or next to nothing, depending on the circumstances). And nope, that's not a typo: service members generally pay zero dollars for healthcare. Many people would say, "Wow, that's a big savings," but if you really think about it, you're actually *making* money. If you have to pay a bill annually because that's a part of the cost of living in a particular society, taking that bill away actually adds value to your overall network. In other words, it's the money that the average American has to put into healthcare costs that you don't. You can put that money into something else. Think about it.

Before I move on to the next benefit, I want to remind you that we only calculated that cost for individuals and not the cost for families, which is roughly $22,000 to $30,000, depending on the circumstances. And no, family members of service members do not have to pay for healthcare either. So a family could be retaining $30,000 in value annually simply by being a service family.

THREE MORE THINGS

I'll make three more points regarding the healthcare benefits of the military and then I'll move on. Truthfully, if you don't see the benefit by now, you probably never will. Here are my last points on healthcare: (1) Unexpected health incidents are covered if you are a service member. (2) Childbirth is covered. (3) Better access to healthcare leads to better health. Trust me when I tell you that all three of these points are benefits that service members take for granted. Not only that, but civilians fail to take notice of them as well.

I will never forget the birth of my beautiful princess. It was the most joyous day of my life. Mommy made it through the birth without corticosteroids and our princess was healthy. As I held my baby girl, all I could do was smile and thank the Lord for his blessing. I was so nervous and excited that I forgot to buy a birthday cake to celebrate our daughter's first day on earth. Yup, buying a birthday cake on your baby's actual birthday is a thing. Why celebrate year one and beyond but not celebrate the actual day? But even without cake, that day was perfect. The weather was beautiful, the vibe was tranquil, our family was grateful...and then the bill came. Yup, the $10,000 "welcome to America" bill. Please don't get me wrong. A child is and will always be priceless, but why pay for something that could be a zero cost benefit? The average birth in America can range anywhere from $8,000 to $40,000 depending on where you are located.[30] Good news for service members is that birth cost is another benefit on the long list of amazing military benefits.

Having unexpected health incidents covered is another important benefit. Let's face it, no one can predict or prevent unexpected health incidents. Sadly, this is just a part of being human. Some people get the luxury of experiencing life without a major health incident; however, the majority of us will experience some sort of unexpected health incident. My big

---

30   "What Does It Cost?," Katy Birth Center, accessed October 17, 2023, https://katybirthcenter.com/what-does-it-cost.

brother was not one of the lucky ones, as he has had a kidney transplant, multiple heart surgeries, and a multitude of other major surgeries. He has spent tens if not hundreds of thousands in personal income and millions in health insurance money. Thankfully, he had good medical insurance, but not everyone is that lucky. Unexpected health costs derail many Americans' career or personal goals and even bankrupt families. For the majority of my readers, healthcare may seem like it doesn't matter because you are young and invincible. My advice to you is don't wait until it starts raining to think about an umbrella.

My last point is better overall quality of life via better healthcare access. Check out this equation: $15,000 annual healthcare cost × seventy-six years (average life span) = $1.14 million total cost for healthcare. That's a lot of coins! Whether you choose to acknowledge it or not, the military offers the best healthcare per cost, period. There is no other company or organization that compares to it. Whether you're seventeen or seventy-six, better healthcare equals a better quality of life. Furthermore, having less financial strain is in itself good for your health. I've experienced my fair share of health scares and also the debt that follows those conditions. Thankfully my military benefits helped me survive many of those incidents. A few years of service could add decades of additional quality of life to your health. Think about it.

CHAPTER 7

★ ★ ★

RETIREMENT WORTH MENTIONING

"Be thankful for what you have: you'll end up having more. If you concentrate on what you don't have you will never, ever have enough."

—OPRAH WINFREY

I remember those days when I used to work for a big electric company doing home theater installations. We would mount TVs, install speakers, set up security cameras, Wi-Fi...You name it, we did it. I remember going to a client's home that overlooked the valley of a neighborhood. I had to fix his security camera in his backyard. I remember thinking to myself, *Man, what does this guy do for a living? This view is crazy!* I felt so at peace in his yard. Shortly after the feeling of peace came a feeling of disappointment. All I could think was, *Man, what am I doing wrong that doesn't allow me to live life like this?* And don't get me wrong, my life wasn't bad at all but it wasn't that. As the troubleshoot continued, he began to open up about his life and eventually revealed that he was a retired service member. He told my partner and me that he did thirty years in the military. He joined at a young age and never saw a reason to leave. He said, "I grew up in the poorest part of New York and worked my way to where I am. I now own a franchised fast food chain and make a good living. I'm retired from the military and I'm enjoying my retirement."

I will never forget how that experience made me feel. It forced me to think about my own retirement. What would it look like? How would I get there? Would it be everything I want it to be? I mean, I had a few dollars in my 401(k) but outside of that had no specific plan.

THE MEANING OF RETIREMENT

What does retirement even mean nowadays? Is it the point when you decide to stop punching the clock? Is it reaching an age where society deems it acceptable to no longer work? Is it after twenty-plus years of working for a company? Or is it just a figment of many Americans' imaginations? Truthfully, I'm not quite sure. The traditional patterns of retirement seem to have disappeared along with the white picket fence. Benefits such as pensions, healthcare through retirement, and complimentary life insurance have all been reduced to companies simply matching your 401(k). In fact, only 4 percent of all companies in the US still offer retirement pensions today compared to 60 percent in 1980.[31] That's terrible! I remember those days when your parents would tell you to just get a good job that has retirement benefits, work hard, and save your money. Man, if only it was still that easy. In today's work environment, you

---

31   "Just How Common Are Defined Benefit Plans?," Ultimate Guide to Retirement, CNN Money, accessed October 17, 2023, https://money.cnn.com/retirement/guide/pensions_basics.moneymag/index7.htm.

have to save for your own retirement. I guess dedicating your lifetime to working for a company is not enough. Something is definitely wrong with that picture. I've seen many of my older family and friends work hard their entire lives just to end up on government assistance, pinching pennies during retirement. In fact, a lot of times that burden ends up falling on the next generation. And the sad thing is no one is trying to fix it. We would have to initiate some serious conscious conversations with our leaders and business owners. But if we can't even get them to talk to each other, why would they talk to us? Either way, if you are interested in a successful retirement, it doesn't get any easier than the military. Here's why.

The first thing to remember before you think about comparing retirement from the military to retirement in the private sector is that only 4 percent of all private-sector companies in the US offer retirement benefits. So technically there is no retirement in America. If you work in the private sector, you're basically on your own. You leave your job with a pat on the back, your 401(k), and whatever title you gained during employment.

Retiring from the military looks very different. But before I dive in, please note that receiving these benefits would require you to complete a minimum of twenty years in the service.

RETIREMENT BENEFITS

The first major benefit is a retirement pension. A pension by definition is a fund into which money is added during an employee's employment years and from which payments are drawn to support that person's retirement.[32] Most private-

---

32   Investopedia Team, "What Is a Pension? Types of Plans and Taxation," Investopedia, updated May 5, 2023, https://www.investopedia.com/terms/p/pensionplan.asp.

sector companies will only offer 401(k) match programs as retirement benefits. With the military, your pension is determined by how many years of service you fulfill. It's calculated at 2.5 percent times your highest thirty-six months of basic pay. For example, if you retired at the minimum of twenty years of service. your retirement pension would be 50 percent of your highest three year pay average. If you wanted to receive 100 percent of your highest three year pay average, you would have to complete forty years of service. Here's an example. Let's say in your last three years of service you made it to E-7. Your average base pay was roughly $5,700 a month. If you were to apply for a retirement pension, you would receive 50 percent of $5,700, which equals $2,850 in basic pension for the rest of your life. I know, I know, that doesn't sound like a lot of money—but remember you only have to do twenty years to qualify for a paycheck for the rest of your life.

Also, if you're the type of person to take your lottery winnings in lump sums, you can do that as well with a military retirement. With the Blended Retirement System, or BRS, service members can choose a lump-sum payment up front over monthly installments. Truthfully, whichever you choose would be a win.

Here is another scenario. Imagine joining the military at seventeen, serving for twenty years, and retiring at thirty-seven. I know thirty-seven sounds old to young folk but trust me, it's young. You won't believe me now but you will when you get older. From thirty-seven until you die, you will be getting paid by the government. Oh and guess what, you can do whatever the heck you want. If you wanted to work in the private sector, you could. If you wanted to start your own business, you could. If you wanted to become a professional grandparent who golfs on their lunch breaks—sure, why not?—you definitely could.

Point is, you can do whatever you want to; you're retired. Remember that only 4 percent of all private-sector jobs offer retirement pension. So honestly, getting anything for retirement is a blessing.

Another benefit of retiring from the military is free relocation. If life's work happened to take you to Europe and you retired there, more than likely you would have to pay to move you and your family back to America. But if you were to retire from the military, the government would pay to move you and your family to the destination of your choice. That's a big difference. Just imagine if you had to pay to move your entire family from, say, Hawaii to Florida. That's kids, clothes, cars, furniture, and everything in between. In fact, the average cost to move a family cross-country ranges from $2,000 to $15,000.[33] So free relocation is a big deal. Take advantage of it. You have up to a year to claim this benefit after retirement.

Another benefit is receiving a military ID for life. This means you can access most military facilities that require military identification. It could be useful if you need to grab a few items from your local base or verify your veteran status.

The next benefit is actually kind of cool. It's called Space-A travel. Space-A or space available is a program that allows retired veterans and their family to fly to any military base in the world for free as long as there is space available. That means you could use US aircrafts as your personal Uber, and the kicker is you don't have to pay for it. That could literally save you thousands of dollars in travel costs.

Transferable healthcare is another great benefit of retiring from the military. If you haven't heard of the government

---

33   Scott Steinberg, "The Average Cost to Move Across the Country: 8 Ways to Save Money," Rocket Mortgage, March 31, 2023, https://www.rocketmortgage.com/learn/cost-to-move-across-the-country.

health insurance known as TRICARE, you've probably been living under a rock. TRICARE is comprehensive medical care for service members, retirees, and their family members.[34] It literally covers everything. Health, dental, hospital visits, and general care for you and your family. When you retire, these health benefits follow you into retirement. All you have to do is pay a small fee annually. The fees are $297 a year for a single person and $594 per year for a family. And don't forget these benefits follow you until death. Furthermore, when you hit the Social Security age of retirement, you no longer have to pay the annual fee. These benefits even apply internationally, to a certain extent.

Two final benefits worth mentioning are survivor benefits and service member burial.

If you happen to pass away, your spouse will receive some of your benefits. This is a good thing: could you imagine being the spouse of an individual who receives benefits, and suddenly they die? You would have to pay for everything on your own. That would be devastating. Thankfully the military has put guidelines in place to protect its veterans and their families.

The last benefit to me is the greatest benefit. If you retire with the military, you automatically qualify for a service member burial. That means if your family chooses, you'll be buried at Arlington National Cemetery, a place that will remain at the forefront of US history for as long as democracy reigns. You'll be put to rest with your brothers and sisters in arms.

---

34   "Tricare 101," Tricare, updated August 24, 2023, https://www.tricare.mil/Plans/New.

THE BIGGEST RETIREMENT BENEFIT

A few weeks ago, I had a huge rash on my back. I had no idea where it came from. I tried to think about what I'd done earlier in the week to see if there was something that caused the rash. Did I touch something? Could it be the new shirt I wore? Was it the visit to the pet store? I just couldn't figure it out. I had no idea why my back had broken out in a rash. But after taking a look in the mirror, I decided to go and get it checked out. I wanted to make sure it wasn't anything crazy like chicken or monkeypox. It was two o'clock in the morning and everyone in the house was asleep. I figured I'd just run to the emergency room really quickly and come right back if it was nothing.

When I got to the ER, I was literally the only person there. It was so quiet that I thought they were closed. The receptionist greeted me with a smile and asked, "How can I help you?" I told her I had broken out with a major rash on my back and had no idea if it was contagious or not. She told me not to worry, the doctor would be there shortly to take a look at it. She did my vitals, checked me in, and told me to hang tight. After about ten minutes or so, the doctor came in and asked to look at my back. She had a carefree look on her face like she had studied for this exam and knew all the answers. She told me to take my shirt off so she could look at my rash. I did and then she laughed and said, "I don't see much here other than some interesting tattoos." I asked the doc if she was sure. She said, "I'm positive. It could've been something that irritated your skin but it's definitely nothing to worry about. I'll prescribe you some topical cream for it. It should go away in a few days." For the average person, this experience would have ended up costing them a few thousand dollars easily. But thanks to the military, my visit to the emergency room was completely free. Trust me when I say this (and I don't say it lightly): in my opinion the

VA is the biggest benefit to service members who retire. The VA not only takes care of veterans' medical needs for retirees, they are also the gatekeepers to a plethora of benefits. Don't worry, I'll break it down in the following chapter.

CHAPTER 8

★ ★ ★

THE VA

"Health is not valued until sickness comes."

—THOMAS FULLER

I remember being a private arriving at the 82nd Airborne Division. I was supposed to go to one of the Brigade Combat Teams but most of them were already deployed. Command had decided to place me and the other new recruits in division headquarters until they figured out what to do with us. Being at division was like being at a summer camp on steroids. It was several barracks full of young men and women with nothing but time and opportunity to get into trouble. Just about every day someone broke some rule that got us "smoked" (disciplined). I did so many push-ups and burpees that they were in my dreams. I had made friends with a private from Texas, a private from Louisiana, and a private from St. Louis. I had a love-hate relationship with the Louisiana kid. He was a cool guy but his judgment wasn't the best. The St. Louis kid was my guy! We were identical in personality and we had the same interests. He was just a little more daring than I was. The kid from Texas was cool, calm, and collected. He was in the background doing his own thing but somehow always seemed to end up in the conversation.

I remember many moments with those guys, but the one thing that I will never forget is when my comrade from Texas told me about the VA. One day we were all shooting the breeze, talking about how much we hated our platoon sergeant. We were mad that he found pleasure in smoking us daily. I said to the guys, "Man, my back is killing me," and everyone agreed that they were in some sort of pain too. The Louisiana kid called us soft and we all laughed.

The private from Texas then said, "Hey, guys, if you're seriously in pain, don't forget to document it."

I said, "Document it? Why?"

"For your VA claim when you get out."

"VA claim? What the heck is that?"

He then went on to explain what the VA was and why it was important to document your injuries and health incidents. He opened my eyes to a benefit I had no idea existed before then. So shout out to all of my Texas folks. I guess everything is bigger in Texas! As I stated before, in my opinion, the VA is the greatest benefit service members receive. Let's take a look into why I feel that way.

Veterans Affairs, also known as the VA, is not just free healthcare for veterans. It's much more than that. The VA administers multiple layers of benefits—so many that I won't be able to cover all of them in this book. However, the key is knowing that these benefits exist to help veterans and their families navigate life during and after their military service. The layers are healthcare, loans, education, compensation, small-business support, life insurance, and death benefits. I'll break them down too.

HEALTHCARE

The average American will spend over $700,000 (uninsured) or roughly $320,000 (insured) on healthcare during the span of their lifetime.[35] Some unfortunate Americans with health conditions will spend millions on their health within that same span. Only God truly knows what the number will be and it's not in his nature to disclose. Regardless, healthcare is an expense that comes with life in the United States. If you're a veteran, this cost could be heavily offset and in many cases completely negated. Any veteran who has served on active duty in a theater of combat operations after 1998 and has been discharged under any other discharge than dishonorable conditions is eligible to receive healthcare at no cost. Furthermore, if you have not served in theater, but have service-connected disabilities rated at 30 percent or more, you are also eligible for healthcare completely free or at a reduced cost. This includes VA facilities and outside network providers. To all of my young readers, this benefit may be going in one ear and out the other, but trust me when I tell you it's important. When you're young you don't think about your health. You think you're Superman or Superwoman. But the older you get, the more you realize you're not as invincible as you thought you were. Your health begins to slip and next thing you know you're the middle-aged neighbor with back pain struggling to keep up with the kids. I'm sure my older readers know exactly what I'm talking about. So, like I said, trust me: document your incidents and injuries, apply for VA, get the benefit now, and use it later, Superman/Superwoman.

---

35   Pete Grieve, "The Lifetime Cost of Health Care Averages $700,000 for Many Insured Americans," Money, November 14, 2022, https://money.com/health-care-costs-lifetime/.

VA LOANS

Another amazing benefit I touched on briefly in the earlier chapters is the VA loan. The VA loan, similar to a signing bonus, is one of the fastest ways to gain wealth through the military. The VA loan allows veterans to purchase real estate without having to deal with all of the red tape the average buyer has to. For example, with the VA loan, a veteran can purchase a home with zero down payment, a lower credit score requirement, a lower interest rate, and no private mortgage insurance (PMI). Furthermore, this is not a one-time deal; this is a lifetime benefit, meaning veterans can use this benefit as many times as they want as long as they follow the guidelines. Let's break these benefits down.

First is the zero down payment. This benefit is huge, and here's why! Did you know that the average cost of a home in America is roughly $430,000?[36] Crazy, right? Sadly, that's the age that we're living in. And if you are trying to buy a home with a traditional loan, the bank requires you to put 20 percent down. Meaning, if you wanted to buy an average house—and we're not even talking about your dream house—you would have to come up with 20 percent of the house value in cash. For those who are not that great at math, 20 percent of $428,000 is $85,600. So if you wanted to buy the average home in America, you would have to come up with $85,000 in cash. I know, that number is almost laughable. I guess you could alway borrow it from Mom or Dad, right? I hate to be the bearer of bad news, but more than likely, Mom and Dad don't have $85,000 in cash to loan you. And truthfully, the majority of the middle class won't have almost $100,000 to loan you either. They will more than likely have to take out a loan or sell one of their assets.

---

36   Jack Caporal, "Average House Price by State in 2023," The Ascent: A Motley Fool Service, updated October 3, 2023, https://www.fool.com/the-ascent/research/average-house-price-state.

Another benefit of the VA loan is the lower interest rate. VA mortgage interest rates are normally anywhere from a quarter to sometimes a whole percentage point lower than a traditional loan. That could save you anywhere from fifty to hundreds of dollars a month on your mortgage, which could end up saving you tens of thousands of dollars over the lifespan of the loan.

The next benefit is no PMI. PMI is private mortgage insurance that most banks require homebuyers to put on their home in order to qualify for a loan. Similar to any other insurance, PMI protects the policyholder if anything were to happen. But let's be clear about a few things. First, PMI does not cover you, the homeowner. It covers the bank. Remember, technically you don't own the home until you pay off the loan. The bank does. So essentially what you are doing when you pay PMI is paying to protect the bank's money—so the bank still gets paid if you can't pay your mortgage. It's a win–win for banks. And to my ears, that sounds like "big bank" taking advantage of "little consumer," but hey, what do I know? Thankfully, the VA protects its veterans from all of this. Here is an example: if you purchase a house for $450,000 and put 10 percent down ($45,000) at an interest rate of 6 percent, your PMI monthly payment would be roughly $105. Now think about what you could do with $105 a month. With PMI you are literally throwing money down the drain. Long story short, with the VA loan you don't have to pay these fees. Thank God! Ultimately, the VA loan keeps money in your pocket—money which, if you're smart, can end up in your investment portfolio. Remember, real estate is and has always been the key to long-term wealth in America. I can guarantee you that every wealthy person on this planet either owns or is invested in real estate. Don't let anyone fool you to believe otherwise. A VA loan can help you get your piece of real estate.

GI BILL

Another life-altering benefit is the GI Bill. I won't elaborate much on this one simply because I've explained it in previous chapters. But as Benjamin Franklin stated, "An investment in knowledge pays the best interest." Education nowadays is one of the most underrated but overvalued assets in America. I know that's a complete contradiction, but think about it. A few decades ago a bachelor's degree was a prestigious accomplishment. Getting a bachelor's back then almost guaranteed you a job. Nowadays, however, a bachelor's degree seems to be more of a vetting tool for businesses, and just another plaque on the wall for graduates. Unsuspecting Americans rack up thousands of dollars of debt and invest countless hours of their time to end up working in a field that has nothing to do with their degree. Don't get me wrong, I'm not saying college is a waste of time. You do learn many practical things that help you navigate adulthood. But I feel there are more efficient ways to get the same experience, like maybe adding an elective class in high school that focuses on life skills. Either way, education is one of the many keys to success, and thanks to the VA, not only can you get it for free but you get paid to go to school. The only thing I would tell those who use the GI Bill is not to settle. Go to the biggest or most prestigious school you can find. Remember, it's free! Also, here are the highlighted benefits of the GI in case you have forgotten:

1. Pays for you to go to school for free
2. Pays for books and supplies
3. Pays you E-5 pay for housing during school
4. Transferable to children
5. Expires after fifteen years of separation (I predict this will change to no expiration)

VA COMPENSATION

I'm gonna tread lightly on this VA benefit; it has a high potential of being misused. Before I begin, I want to make sure that I am clear on this: it is an honor to serve in the military. If you are simply joining the military for benefits, cool. I'm not mad at that. Not everyone comes in for the same reason. However, if you join the military to get a check from the VA, you are wrong. Not only are you wrong but you are committing a crime. It's called fraud.

VA compensation in short is the government paying you for your health decline during your time in service. Here's an example: let's say you went into the military with a clean bill of health. You completed three years of service and came out not as healthy as you were when you went in. Your back is not as strong due to heavy lifting and daily exercising. Your sleep has become inconsistent due to the stress of training and you now experience anxiety when you're in crowded places. So just for simplicity's sake, let's say your bill of health went from 100 percent to 60 percent due to these new health conditions you've developed. You are technically still healthy, you can still work, and you function fine within society; however, you're not the young whippersnapper you were. With VA compensation, the government will pay you for your health decline. So that 40 percent decline in health will become a compensation check you will receive for the rest of your life.

The benefit is huge. If you really think about it, everyone, regardless of where they work or who they work for, will see their health decline over time. It's called gravity! Other physically intense careers do not offer a benefit as such. You only get lifetime pay for an injury or health incident if you file some sort of lawsuit. Outside of that, you'll be nursed back to what they deem a suitable state then left to put all the pieces back together on your own. VA compensation is an amazing benefit set aside for an amazing group of people. Don't abuse it.

LIFE INSURANCE

Have you ever watched A&E's *Cold Case Files* or *The First 48*? If you haven't, I'll give you the rundown. Normally there's an unsuspecting person living a normal life, then all of a sudden they are murdered. They had no known enemies, were happily married, and had no suspicious activity that would lead to murder. There is no obvious motive. The victim was a hardworking person and was loved by their community. They worked their way up the ladder and sadly didn't get to enjoy the life that success brings. Then, after doing some digging, the cops find out that the main person of interest is actually the closest person to the victim. Long story short, they come to find out the victim's spouse murdered them for their life insurance policy.

I remember speaking to my financial adviser and he said something that really stuck with me. He said, "Delano, try not to be worth more dead than alive." I laughed but knew exactly what he was referring to. Let's face it: no one wants to talk about life insurance. For some strange reason people think when you talk about life insurance you're plotting their death. Trust me, I know: my family is extremely superstitious about it. Every time I have a conversation with them, they look at me like, *Yeah, I know* or *Man, that sounds great but I'm good. You are not gonna have me knocked off for some life insurance policy.* Guys and gals, even though this is somewhat of a laughable mentality, it's wrong. For too many years, families have blocked the transfer of generational wealth due to the fear of life insurance. My answer for scared or superstitious people is "just don't tell anyone!"

You can literally stay silent. They'll find out when you're dead and they'll thank you.

Long story short, the transfer of wealth is simple and affordable via military life insurance policies. The VA has several insurance policies that are definitely worth exploring. Here are a couple:

- Servicemembers' Group Life Insurance (SGLI) is life insurance coverage for active-duty service members that has a basic premium rate of six cents per $1,000 of insurance coverage.[37] A monthly premium will be automatically taken out of your basc pay to cover your policy. This premium also includes an additional $1 per month for Traumatic Injury Protection coverage (TSGLI).
- Veterans' Group Life Insurance (VGLI) is life insurance coverage for veterans not on active duty or special assignment. VGLI premium rates are based on your age and the amount of insurance coverage you want. For example, if you're twenty-nine or younger you can receive a $500,000 policy for $35 a month. You spend more on coffee and cigarettes, if that's still a thing.

Look into it, guys. It's important! Just don't disclose it if you're superstitious.

DEATH BENEFITS

I'll name a few death benefits to get you going. First, veterans receive the option to be buried in a national cemetery. If a

---

37 "Servicemembers' Group Life Insurance (SGLI)," US Department of Veterans Affairs, updated March 1, 2023, https://www.va.gov/life-insurance/options-eligibility/sgli.

veteran chooses, they can be buried next to their brothers and sisters in arms. Their family will forever know that they honor them by serving their country. The family will also receive a burial flag, which stands as a symbol of gratitude for their loved one's sacrifice. To add to that, the VA actually pays for the service and arrangements for the veteran's burial.

I remember watching the movie *Saving Private Ryan* and breaking down in tears. It was the cemetery scene and Harrison Richard Young was honoring his fallen comrades. The scene brought back every emotion I've ever buried. I understood the pain and sacrifice those veterans went through while serving their country. They bore a burden many ran from. Right then and there, I told my family I would like to be buried in one of our many national cemeteries. They acknowledged my request and agreed to honor it. We all have to go one day; when I'm gone I want to be laid to rest with my brothers in arms. I want my daughter to know that her father was a part of something bigger than himself. Thankfully, the VA affords me this great benefit.

The other benefit worth mentioning is the VA dependent and survivor benefits. Upon your death the VA transfers a percentage of your benefits to your family members. Your spouse and children will receive compensation, education, and health benefits just as you did.

In my opinion, the VA is by far the biggest benefit the military has to offer, and I know that is a big statement for me to make, especially given all the amazing benefits I've listed already. The reason I believe the VA is best of all is the *amount* of benefits you receive, and also the age at which you can receive the benefits. In many other careers (and you can look at hundreds or thousands of career fields), when an individual decides to leave they normally leave with their 401(k), whatever savings they have, and their work title. Here's an example. Let's say you were in banking. You dedicated your life to banking because that was your dream and your passion. You did that for twenty years and made it to bank manager. Sadly, once you decide to leave the bank you'll leave with whatever you put in your 401(k) and your fancy position title. Oh, and don't forget about the big fancy pat on the back for dedicating your life to that company. With the military and the VA, you not only get a pat on the back and get to keep your job title, you also get a lifetime of benefits. I'll tell you like my recruiter told me: you get a lifetime of benefits for a few years of service. As the Italians say, *"Think about it!"*

CHAPTER 9

★ ★ ★

ADDITIONAL BENEFITS

"I have legally used the tax laws to my benefit and to the benefit of my company, my investors, and my employees. I mean, honestly, I have brilliantly—I have brilliantly used those laws."

—DONALD TRUMP

Donald Trump is the most publicized president in modern history. His ability to leverage his strengths to maximize results is truly something to awe over. As Americans, I'm sure we'll never agree on his policies, but we can all agree that the former president is good *at what he does*. It's up to you to determine if what he's doing is good or bad. The point is to always maximize your strengths.

SOMETHING I NEVER REALIZED

I remember sitting at my dining room table one night and staring at the surface of the table. It was an eight-foot reclaimed-wood table that I just loved, but I wasn't staring because I was in awe. I was staring because I was lost in thought, trying to figure out what expenses I could cut back on in order to help finance my startup business. As I went through each bill, I got to my daughter's school fee. It was nearly $300 a week. All I could think was, *Man, that's the cost of a small condo.* But when I decided to look deeper into my daughter's school fee, I noticed that we weren't even paying full price. We were actually getting 20 percent off (military discount), a savings of $75 a week. Add that up and we had actually saved $3,600 a year. It hit me like a ton of bricks. I then asked myself, *How much money have I actually saved due to military discounts?* I'd never thought of it. It never crossed my mind. Normally I would just ask and if a company offered a discount I would think to myself, *Sweet!* Military discounts outside of what the government offers are huge cost-saving benefits. However, most veterans ignore them or don't give them the credit they deserve. They could save you thousands in out-of-pocket costs and could actually be seen as financial gains.

I'll give you another example. Let's say Jimmy works at Best Buy, where he receives an employee discount on electronics at 10 percent above cost. Jimmy is a tech guru and has spent thousands of dollars on electronics over the years. In fact, between birthdays, holidays, and the latest iPhone release, Jimmy spends roughly $6,000 a year. The issue isn't Jimmy's spending, it's his lack of saving. Don't worry, I'll explain. Jimmy spent $6,000 after his discount savings. But once he did the math, he realized that he would have spent approximately $10,000 without the discount. The problem is, Jimmy didn't maximize his strengths by investing the money he saved. Instead of looking at his discount as a gain in his savings or investment account, he simply looked at the cost of the product after the discount. In other words, Jimmy doesn't pay himself the discounted savings; he puts it back into his general account, ultimately not maximizing his discount.

Employee discounts are benefits that many employees take for granted. They don't see them as a major benefit of employment. People look at what they are saving but don't realize it translates into gains as well. If you save $500 on an employee discount, you technically made $500 because, truth be told, you would have spent the money either way. The discount just makes the pill easier to swallow. People tend to look at it backward: *I'm saving money but I'm not making money*. In my opinion, when you save on an item you would have bought either way, you're actually making money.

I'll break that down a little more. Things that you need for your home—e.g., light bulbs, AC filters, groceries, gas, and other essential items—are normal costs associated with daily life. They are there and you have to pay for them whether you like it or not. Therefore, if you are getting those items at a discount you are actually gaining in the long run. I'm sure there is a term for this, but truthfully I don't care much about terms; it's more about making sure you understand the concept.

I said all of that to say this: your military service affords you the opportunity to receive discounts on many items and from many retailers. Service members not only need to be aware of companies that give military discounts but need to understand the benefit of those discounts. To keep it straight and plain, military discounts equal net gains. The majority of major retailers offer 10 percent off for veterans. Some can go up to higher discounts but 10 percent seems to be the norm. Let's now compare that to a civilian job. With a civilian gig, you are eligible for a discount with that employer and that employer only. With the military, you have access to discounts with hundreds of businesses and companies. So in a sense, doing three years in the military is like working three years for *hundreds* of companies—because once you're a veteran you now receive a discount on merchandise from hundreds of different companies. On the civilian side of things, if you work for a car manufacturer, you get the manufacturer's discount; however, once you leave you no longer qualify for that discount. Think about that for a sec. Also, can you imagine going into a store that you've never contributed to and receiving benefits? That's crazy! But that's one of your many benefits as a service member.

Now let's do some math. We'll use Home Depot as an example. The average American spends approximately $1,052 a year at Home Depot.[38] The life expectancy of the average American is seventy-seven years. If we're being realistic, the average individual would probably start shopping at Home Depot at the age of sixteen because that's their age of employment. And most senior citizens don't stop shopping for themselves until between the ages of eighty and ninety. So from age sixteen to seventy-seven, the average American more than likely still shops at Home Depot. That's sixty-one years. If you multiply sixty-one years by $1,052, the average American spends $64,172 at Home Depot. Now, if you were to apply Home Depot's military discount, you would have saved roughly $6,400 (or as I like to put it, *gained* $6,400) just for being a veteran—and that's only one store.

Here is something else that may blow your mind. According to savingadvice.com, the average American household spends $3.6 million over their lifetime.[39] If you were to apply a 10 percent discount over an individual's lifetime, they would have

---

38 Dominick Reuter, "The Typical Home Depot Customer Is a 45-Year-Old White Man with a College Degree Earning Over $80,000," Business Insider, February 21, 2023, https://www.businessinsider.com/typical-home-depot-shopper-demographic-middle-aged-white-man-2021-8.

39 Tamila McDonald, "You Won't Believe How Much Money the Average American Spends in a Lifetime," SavingAdvice.com, August 17, 2022, https://www.savingadvice.com/articles/2022/08/17/1098057_you-wont-believe-how-much-money-the-average-american-spends-in-a-lifetime.html.

saved $360,000—or as I like to put it, they would have *gained* $360,000. Think about it!

Before I wrap up this chapter, there's one final point I'd like to make. Currently, there are still too many companies that do *not* honor military discounts. What is their excuse? How difficult is it to honor a veteran by providing them with 10 percent off the item they are purchasing? It truly bothers me when I walk into a store to purchase an item and the store owner says, "We don't offer military discounts but thank you for your service." What's the point of dry thanking someone when you could express your thanks through action? One of my life's goals is to help facilitate the passing of legislation that mandates all businesses to grant service members a 10 percent discount. That's the least we can do for our service members. Note: I have included a huge list of outlets that offer military discounts at the end of the book. I did that for two reasons: (1) to help you take advantage of your benefits, and (2) to open your eyes to the countless benefits available to service members. My rule of thumb is to always ask for a military discount. The worst that could happen is the company saying that they don't offer one.

CHAPTER 10

★ ★ ★

THE BLUEPRINT

"He who fails to plan is planning to fail."

—SIR WINSTON CHURCHILL

High school gym class, another boring day in physical education (PE). I loved working out but hated everything in between. Our gym teacher, normally consumed by one of the student athletes, rarely interacted with the rest of the class—until that one day. One day, he rolled out an old tube TV that looked like it was on its last leg. He plugged it in and put on the news. The anchor was rather calm. She spoke to her audience saying, "Ladies and gentlemen, it seems as though the World Trade Center has been hit by a small aircraft of some sort and is currently on fire. Firefighters have been dispatched to the scene and are currently helping with the incident." To be honest, at the time I had no idea what the World Trade Center was. I figured it was just some big building in New York and all buildings were big in New York. I was confused as to why of all things our PE teacher decided to put that on for us to watch. As we all looked on wondering what the heck was happening, another airplane came out of nowhere and slammed into the second tower. Upon impact, some of the students in the classroom screamed, yelling out, "Oh no!" My heart dropped. I didn't know what to say or do. I was shell-shocked. The news anchor went from calm to frantic, screaming, "Oh my god, oh my god, I think we're being attacked!"

I remember being confused, not really knowing what was happening or how to respond. We watched the news for the next hour, watching both towers fall, watching people jump out of the World Trade Center, falling to their deaths. At some point during the second tower falling, our teacher had stepped out of the classroom. He came back yelling, "Okay, everyone call your parents to pick you up, class is dismissed!" The news anchor's words—"We're being attacked"—replayed in my head over and over. I was angry. I had tears in my eyes but didn't know why. The only reference of attack or war I knew was Pearl Harbor, the battle for Europe, the Pacific battles, and Vietnam. You know, the stuff that plays on the History Channel. As we began to pour out of the classrooms, I wondered if Japanese Zero fighters would come down from the sky and try to pick us off one by one. All I could think of was those people stuck in those towers. I remember thinking, *Man, all of those people are gone. Why would anyone want to do something like that? People hate America that much?* Apparently they do and I had no idea! Ultimately, that day changed my life forever.

THE UNFORTUNATE TRUTH ABOUT AMERICA

I said all of that to say this. Americans have become so hypersensitive to the idea of patriotism. Lately it seems as though everyone hates America. Even some of the citizens that enjoy her great benefits. Please don't think that I'm saying America is perfect. We all know there's work to be done. But it seems as though we seek out our differences and ignore our similarities. Polar opposite cultures and a lack of unity within our government seem to be the usual culprits for such discord. However, I truly believe that America is a great concept—and can be an amazing reality. We just have to work together. I have to say, as tragic as 9/11 was, it was the first time in decades Americans were simply just that, Americans. There was no black, no white, no left, no right. We were all angry, all hurt—but we were all in it together. We wanted justice and we wanted it now.

As I've stated before, and it bears repeating: this book isn't just about going into the military to take advantage of some government benefits. Joining the military is an honor. In fact, it should be a gesture of appreciation for your country. Yes, the benefits are going to change your life and help create generational wealth. But you should also take pride in being part of the solution and not the problem. I know there are many Americans who would say, "I'm not slaving for Uncle Sam." This isn't about Uncle Sam (whoever that's supposed to be) or whoever you think is trying to manipulate you. This is about you doing your part to protect your America, whatever that may be. I tell anti-military people all the time, if the military did not defend our freedom, would we even have the freedom to say what we dislike? There are countries around the world that would love to see the demise of America. They couldn't care less where you're from and what you like or dislike. It doesn't matter if you're from Mississippi or Florida, Texas or California, New York or the Virgin Islands, Hawaii or Puerto Rico. They don't discriminate. The death of any American would suffice. So please let's stop making America's real enemies' jobs easier. The point is, it's an honor to serve and you should be proud to do so.

THINGS TO PREPARE FOR

Joining the military comes with great benefits, but as reggae artist Buju Banton would sing, it's "not an easy road." The military is extremely structured, which will require discipline. Being that it's a conglomerate of hierarchies, it will also demand respect for authority, or at bare minimum adherence to authority. It will require you to put your pride aside. There will be peer pressure, and possibly pressure from leadership, for you to not rock the boat. Last, there will be tons of idle time where if you're not careful you could pick up a bad habit or two. Remember, as a civilian you're used to doing your own thing, but in the military there is no "I" or doing "my thing." Well, at least when you're on duty. So, if you're considering taking my advice and joining, now would be a good time to start shifting your mindset.

MILLIONAIRE MINDSET

If you've made it to this chapter, congratulations. Believe it or not, you likely have what it takes to change your generation for the better. Did you know that 23 percent of Americans haven't read a book (not even part of one) in the past year[40] and that 85 percent of self-made millionaires read books?[41] Looks like you're in good company. Former UK Prime Minister Winston Churchill said something I'll never forget: "He who fails to plan, plans to fail." In other words, you can have all the mindset, all

---

40 Risa Gelles-Watnick and Andrew Perrin, "Who Doesn't Read Books in America?," Pew Research Center, September 21, 2021, https://www.pewresearch.org/short-reads/2021/09/21/who-doesnt-read-books-in-america.

41 Anirbar Kar, "Reading Is More Important Than You Think—Here's Why!," Books Are Our Superpower (blog), Medium, October 5, 2020, https://baos.pub/reading-is-more-important-than-you-think-heres-why-24128b47f630.

the knowledge, all the ambition, all the resources, but if you don't have a plan, you don't have a play. It's like being in the Super Bowl and your coach tells you to forget the game plan and just play ball. I'm pretty sure you would look at them crazy and then proceed to cuss them the heck out. Well, you wouldn't be wrong. A play is nothing without a plan. Now, like Jay-Z's sixth album, welcome to the blueprint, a.k.a. the plan.

THE BLUEPRINT

The blueprint is a step-by-step plan for individuals who are not sure what to do in order to get the most out of their time in service. Again, like with everything in this book, it is not a get-rich-quick scheme nor will it guarantee success. (Truthfully, I do believe it will but I said that for the idiots that like to sue.) Now let's begin.

1. SAVE YOUR SIGNING BONUS

First things first: a military signing bonus is one of the quickest opportunities—or as some folks would say, "fastest come up"—you'll ever have to gain wealth. You literally go from no money to tens of thousands of dollars in a matter of months. If you weren't paying attention to my first couple of chapters, I'll say it again. As a service member you literally have a bigger signing bonus than most rappers. The problem is that, like many of my army buddies, most people blow their signing bonus as fast as they get it. Cars, clothes, and buying love is normally what dries that well for most service members. I've seen service members spend their signing bonus on vehicles, designer clothes, women, men, and whatever else they feel will give them temporary gratification. Trust me when I tell you this: don't spend your signing bonus. Don't end up like Johnny No Cash. You could literally double your money instead of blowing it. Here's an example. Let's say you got a $50,000 signing bonus. You put all $50,000 in an automated investment account. That investment earns you roughly 13 percent annually. So you start your time in service with $50,000 courtesy of your signing bonus and leave with $74,000. And that example is one of you just playing it safe. If you got more aggressive, you could make two to three times that amount in profits. Don't forget also that you would only be twenty years old. You joined at seventeen. Hold on to that $74,000. I'll tell you what to do with it in a minute.

2. SET A SPENDING BUDGET DURING YOUR ENLISTMENT

Okay, so look: I know you have to eat, live, and enjoy your time in service to the best of your abilities, but remember, you went in for a purpose and that purpose was to leave better off than you came in. I'm not telling you to be a barracks rat, but I am saying you will have to do some intentional saving. Let's take a look at some numbers. The average E-2 makes roughly $25,000 a year in base pay alone. Remember, this does not include additional pay such as housing or food allowance. So if we were to break down that $25,000, it equals about $2,000 a month. Realistically, you should only need about $1,400 of that $2,000 in order to live comfortably during your time in service. Now let's add that difference up: $600 ×12 months = $7,200 × 3 years = $21,600. Now, if you were to put that into an investment account that brought you 13 percent annually, you would be taking home about $25,000. If you were to add the $25,000 to your signing bonus profits of $74,000, you would technically be a six-figure individual with $99,000 in your investment accounts. And the great thing is you don't have to do anything crazy like eat canned food, cancel your favorite streaming subscriptions, or stop buying your favorite coffee every morning. You can literally live your life and enjoy your military experience while you build wealth. You can still go out, buy things, and even still party if you like, as long as you remember to put that $600 away. This is a perfect example of how your money can *make* money for you—and believe it or not, we're just getting started.

3. DO NOT BUY A VEHICLE

This next guideline in the blueprint is something everyone struggles with for some reason. If you can overcome this, you'll be better off than most. Please, please, please, whatever you do, do not go out and buy a new vehicle. If you already own a vehicle, keep the one you have. If you don't have a vehicle and honestly don't need one, do not throw money into a vehicle. If you don't understand why, I'll explain in a second. But first things first: if you have children or a situation that requires a vehicle, then by all means get a vehicle. But if you live in the barracks, don't have responsibilities that require a vehicle, and don't live outside of the military base radius, trust me, do not buy a vehicle! Here's why. Most military bases have everything a service member needs either on base or a short distance away. Furthermore, just about every service member either has a vehicle or ends up buying one. Here's what ends up happening. You have twenty soldiers with twenty vehicles all parked outside in the barracks parking lot. And when the guys and gals at the barracks go out, nine times out of ten they carpool. So someone's expensive new car, truck, sedan, coupe, SUV, or motorcycle always ends up sitting in the lot. Furthermore, a car is like a kid: you pay for them even after they can pay for themselves. Meaning, after you take the vehicle home you still have to pay for it regardless of whether you paid cash, leased, or financed. Here is a little equation I came up with to help you understand what I'm saying:

vehicle + you = unnecessary spending (gas + insurance + maintenance) > your money = broke for no reason

You'll go broke because you have to pay taxes, interest, gas, insurance, and maintenance for something that's gonna be sitting in the barracks parking lot most of the time. Some people would say, "You could be saving a lot of money." I say, "You could be *making* a lot of money." Remember, all of the money you would have spent on your vehicle could have been going into your pockets or into your $99,000 investment account. So as hip-hop artist Big Boi from the group Outkast said, "Now marinate on that for a minute."

4. USE YOUR TUITION ASSISTANCE

One of the biggest missed opportunities I see from service members is not taking advantage of their TA or tuition assistance. Soldiers, Sailors, Marines, Airmen, Guardsman, and everyone in between all drop the ball when it comes to TA. Tuition assistance pays service members up to $4,500 per calendar year to go to school.[42] However, for some reason, everyone focuses on their post-military education benefit and not the one they have during their time in service. Ladies and gentlemen,

---

42 "Tuition Assistance (TA)," My Army Benefits, reviewed June 28, 2023, https://myarmybenefits.us.army. mil/Benefit-Library/Federal-Benefits/Tuition-Assistance-(TA)?serv=122#:~:text=The%20Tuition%20 Assistance%20(TA)%20Program,and%20personal%20self%2Ddevelopment%20goals.

take advantage of your TA. Do not wait until you get out of the service to start your education journey. If you do not have a degree, this is your opportunity to get an associate's degree or go to trade school and pick up a certification. You can even start your bachelor's program and finish it once you get out. Trust me, take advantage of the free education. And yes, you'll thank me later. Instead of going out and partying or just heading back to the barracks to play video games and drink, you should take advantage of the tuition assistance and use it to your benefit. Stop using the excuse of not having time, your program not being offered, your command not supporting you, or that you have a job outside of duty. People who get things done don't make excuses. So get it done!

5. DOCUMENT YOUR INJURIES WHILE YOU'RE ON DUTY

I hate begging for things for myself but don't mind begging if it benefits someone else. Current and future service members, please, please, please document all of your health incidents during your time in service. Notice I used the phrase "health incidents" and not "injuries." That wasn't by mistake. There is a difference. An injury is somewhat self-explanatory. You break a bone, that's an injury. You pull a tendon, that's an injury. A health incident, on the other hand, could be something like you notice that every time you go to the mall you panic or have a hard time breathing. Another one could be, you notice that you've started getting headaches or nosebleeds and you've never had either before. Sadly, many service members do not document their health incidents, which eventually become health conditions years after they have completed their time in service. And similar to history, if you do not document it, it technically never happened. Not documenting history is an old trick many societies have used to take advantage of the oppressed. Don't let it happen to you. Document everything, and I mean everything.

There are two reasons that service members don't document their injuries or health incidents:

1. **Macho man/woman mentality:** "I'm a service machine! I never get hurt. I can do this all day!" If you're not strong enough to tell your sergeant that your knee, back, or neck is killing you, then you're not as strong as you think. Another big missed opportunity soldiers have is not reporting incidents. Instead of reporting, you listen to your macho sergeant who is all gung ho. He or she tells you, "Oh, your back is hurting, you'll be fine, just walk it off or go get a massage." If you're one of those people who follow the crowd by staying silent, you'll never get ahead in life. You'll always be the follower and most importantly, when your heydays are gone and reality settles in, you won't be able to receive the benefits you earned because like many oppressors, you erased your own history.

2. **Unawareness:** This second reason many service members do not document their health incidents is just as bad as the first. They simply don't know they need to. Sadly, many service members are clueless as to the benefits they are eligible to receive if their health incidents turn into health conditions. I've seen it personally and have also experienced it myself. Many times I've had a really bad health incident but ignored it because I figured it didn't matter. But it's not too late for you. So as I said in the beginning, please document your health incidents and injuries. Remember, if it's not documented it never happened. I don't like writing in all caps but this is necessary: *PLEASE DOCUMENT EVERY*

MEDICAL INCIDENT YOU EXPERIENCE WHILE IN THE MILITARY. It's going to be important when you get out.

6. INVEST IN THE THRIFT SAVINGS PLAN

A Thrift Savings Plan (TSP) is very similar to a civilian 401(k): you put your money in and the government matches your money then invests it for you. The good thing about these accounts is that you can turn the aggressiveness up or down depending on what you want.

Here are a couple benefits of the TSP just in case you didn't know:

1. TSP comes out of your paycheck before taxes. That means you get to do what the rich do, which is avoid taxes. Meaning, to the IRS you look like you have less money than you actually do, which will result in Big Brother taking less of your money during tax time.

2. The government matches your TSP up to 5 percent. So, if you did nothing at all with your TSP, you would at minimum earn 5 percent plus whatever the market gains are for those years. Just to give you a little perspective, the average savings account earns 0.46 percent. That's not even 1 percent. So even before adding capital gains, the TSP earns you roughly 500 percent more than your bank savings account would. That's insane! There are a couple other benefits like lower fees and more investment customization, but honestly nothing worth mentioning. The big benefit is matching your money. Now let's take a look at some numbers. Let's say you're an E-3 making $27,000 a year in base pay. You put 5 percent of your $27,000 annually ($2,250 monthly) into your TSP and the government automatically matches you

at 5 percent. That's $112 a month of your money plus $112 of the government's match money. That $224 ×12 months = $2,688. Add market gains at 13 percent over three years and that's $9,480. I know what you're thinking: it's only nine grand. But just remember, millionaires that get their wealth all at once normally don't keep it. Real wealth builds over time. Furthermore, if you were to add that $9,000 to your $99,000 you would officially be a six-figure individual at $108,000.

7. EVERY TIME YOU GET PROMOTED, PUT THE DIFFERENCE INTO YOUR INVESTMENT ACCOUNT

You started off saving $600 as an E-2. But when you hit the pay grade of E-3, you know you'll be making approximately $110 more each month. Take that money and add it to your $600 savings budget. That should bring your total savings for your investment account up to roughly $710 a month. Then, when you get to the pay grade of E-4, rinse and repeat and now you'll be saving $954 a month. That's almost a thousand bucks a month. This step is very important: it's called paying yourself. Give yourself a savings increase as you get promoted. It's a normal thing that smart people do with their money.

8. STAY IN THE BARRACKS

If you're single and your pay grade is below E-6, you are eligible to stay in the barracks if your unit has space. I know you've probably heard some crazy stories about life in the barracks. I know how you feel because I've been there. I remember being in the barracks and sharing a room with another soldier. To make matters worse, we shared the bathroom with the entire floor. It was so weird because our room layout was two beds in a ten-by-ten-foot room with two gym lockers, a window, and a door. We ended up putting a few ponchos together to create bedrooms. I remember talking on the phone and forgetting my roommate was there, then all of a sudden he started laughing, saying, "Bro, your mom is funny." I couldn't even do what single people tend to do on the internet because my roommate was literally right on the other side of my poncho. But as weird as that was, I would do it all over again. I would stay in the barracks, because it helped me build my wealth. Also, to be fair, this was 2006 and they were in the middle of transitioning to the "new barracks." In fact, a year later I was transferred to the new barracks where we had a key card and our own room with a living room and kitchen. It was fancy! But like I said, trust me, stay in the barracks even if you're more comfortable in a place of your own. Why? Similar to kids and a vehicle, you will have to pay for your place of residence until it can pay for itself. That's rent, lights, water, insurance, maintenance, and everything else that comes with living on your own. Most savings accounts pay for themselves; most apartments are paid for with savings. Marinate on that for a minute.

9. EAT AT THE DINING FACILITY

Why would you pay to eat when you can eat breakfast, lunch, and dinner for free? Similar to the barracks, single E-5 and below do not have to pay to eat at the Dining Facility (DFAC). This is huge! Here's the proof. Did you know that the average American spends an estimated $150 to $300 a week on food?[43]

---

43   "Food Budgets: How Much Your Monthly Food Budget Should Be + Grocery Calculator," Mint, updated September 28, 2022, https://mint.intuit.com/blog/food-budgets/monthly-grocery-budget-calculator.

Think about it. You go to your favorite spot and order breakfast; that's more than likely $10. You get lunch; that's roughly $15. You order a pizza for dinner; that's $20. You've already spent $45 and it's only Monday. Multiply that $45 by seven days and you've spent $315. Like Hov (Shawn Carter) said, "Man lie, woman lie, numbers don't." Do the math! The issue most service members have with the DFAC is that it's not cool to eat with the privates (rookies) once you have passed a certain rank. Well, let me tell you something, soldier: cool isn't paying you; you're paying to be cool. Plus, this is a short-term task. You're not doing twenty years. You don't have time to waste on trying to look cool. Focus on your task at hand and get the job done. Be smart and maximize your time and money while you're in the military.

10. GO TO AS MANY SCHOOLS AND TRAINING AS YOUR UNIT WILL ALLOW

Your chain of command determines who gets to go to which schools. Talk to your chain of command to find out if there are any schools available for you to attend. Most of the schools are fairly short and pretty easy. Adding military schools to your résumé will help you get promoted faster, gain an advantage with your chain of command, and also bolster your civilian résumé. I took advantage of school and courses during my time in service and it helped me get to the rank of sergeant in two years. Examples of school and training are airborne school; air assault school; flight training; Jumpmaster School; Pathfinder School; Survival, Escape, Resistance, and Evasion (SERE) school; Master Driver Course; and many more. I'll be honest, going to additional military schools is not for everyone. Also, if you decided to skip this step, honestly you would still be okay. But if you're looking for an edge over your competition, I recommend doing additional courses.

11. IF YOU DECIDE TO STAY OFF BASE, NEVER RENT

Another big mistake many service members make is putting their wealth in the hands of others. Think about it: why pay someone else when you can pay yourself? Many service members think that because they're not going to be in a particular area for a long time, that means they should rent. The problem with that mentality is that you are literally handing your wealth to someone else. Stop using that you won't be there long as an excuse. The truth is your landlord more than likely doesn't live in that state either. Why would you give them your money when you can give it to your child, your spouse, or yourself? If more service members had the mentality of owning where they lived, the wealth of the military would stay with our veterans. Think about it! Plus, home ownership for veterans is an extremely easy process. It's zero down, with an average credit score of 620.[44] So excuses are limited. Also, you can use housing allowance to pay the mortgage on the house—so technically the military is paying for your brand-new house. And when you're ready to leave, you can rent it out to another service member or sell it if the profits are good enough (I personally wouldn't recommend selling, however).

44 Tim Alvis, "VA Loan Credit Score Minimums and Lender Requirements for 2023," Veterans United Home Loans, July 31, 2023, https://www.veteransunited.com/realestate/va-loans-and-credit-score-minimums-what-all-buyers-need-to-know.

12. PAY OFF ALL YOUR DEBT—DON'T UPGRADE YOUR LIFESTYLE TO YOUR NEW PAYCHECK

If you came into the military with debt, please do not leave the military with the same or more debt. The military's Soldiers and Sailors Civil Relief Act (SCRA) is a great benefit that service members can take advantage of during their time in service. With SCRA a service member can get mortgage relief, help with lease terminations, protection from eviction, lower interest rates, and a few other benefits. Furthermore, with all the income and savings you're receiving from the military, it would behoove you to pay off your debt. That's because, truth be told, it's going to be ten times harder to pay it off when you finish your time in service.

13. KNOW WHAT YOU WANT TO DO BEFORE YOU GET OUT OF THE MILITARY

Man, I've seen so many service members, including myself, waste years after exiting the service trying to figure out what they want to do. Don't wait until you get out to start making a plan. That makes no sense. You should be exploring your options while you're still in the military, trying new things, volunteering in fields that interest you. Trust me, it will save you and your family years of hurrying up and waiting while Mr./Mrs. "I didn't do this while I was in service" figures out what they want to do. Let's say you want to go to law school. You should be thinking, *What can I do now, while I'm still in the military, to help me get my law degree?* Start prepping in year one of service and by the time you get out, you will be ready for your journey.

14. SIGNING BONUS AND SAVINGS—NEVER KEEP MONEY IN A REGULAR SAVINGS ACCOUNT

Inflation has killed all savings accounts. At this point, putting your money into a savings account will actually cost you money. If you were not aware, banks use your money to make money. They take your money and invest it, loan it out to people, and charge them interest. Why should the bank capitalize off of your money? Invest in stocks, mutual funds, or bonds. Average yields are 13 percent.[45] Thirteen percent should be enough to fight off inflation. Other good options are short-term certificates of deposit (CDs). They're good interest makers but don't lock your money away too long. Also, invest in the stock market or real estate. Even if they crash, history has proven that they always come back. Last thing: if you've never invested before, I do not advise you doing so on your own. Speak to a financial advisor or an elder you trust.

15. COLLEGE—THINK BIGGER

This one definitely gets me every time. I've never understood how service members with a full ride through college end up going to a community college. And just to clarify, there is nothing wrong with community college. I've been there and done that. But if the government is paying for you to attend any public university within your state, why wouldn't you go to the best school your money can buy? I've seen service members waste their GI Bill on community college and then years later end up paying to finish their education at a state university.

---

45   Liz Kneuven, Rickie Houston, and Tessa Campbell, "Average Stock Market Return Over the Past 10 Years," Business Insider, September 18, 2023, https://www.businessinsider.com/personal-finance/average-stock-market-return.

I get that many service members may feel they're not qualified to attend the top university in their state. However, I challenge you to challenge yourself. Here's my personal example: I went to a local college because it was safe. It was within my comfort zone. I knew I couldn't fail or be rejected. But I ended up wasting two years of my GI Bill going through the motions at this college. I didn't feel like a bum but I wasn't proud of myself. I was content. As I got older, I started coaching scholastic sports and was afforded the opportunity to visit different local colleges and universities. After my visits I realized the kids at the top universities were no different than the kids at community college. In fact, in some instances the kids at the community college were smarter than the kids at the big universities. The big university kids just had more preparation, confidence, and funding. At that moment, I realized that all kids are pretty much the same; it's just that some have more preparation than others.

That semester I finished my degree at the smaller university and applied to one of the most prestigious universities in my state. That changed my life. I was able to rub shoulders with affluent people and build networks beyond my neighborhood. Surrounded by kids with expectations changed my expectations and goals. I will never forget the time I was talking to a fellow student about my investment account. I told her I was considering putting a few thousand in a company that was making a comeback in the stock market. She said with a carefree demeanor, "Oh, really? Nice! My dad just gave me $225,000 to invest in the market. I think I'm going to invest in Amazon."

My mind was blown. I smiled and said, "Oh, okay, nice," but I was stunned by her resources. I had $30,000 to invest and I thought I was rich. She had $225,000 and could care less. The average student at my university paid $225,000 for tuition. I got

it for free. *GO TO THE BEST SCHOOL WITHIN YOUR STATE.*
Don't settle for community college.

16. WHAT TO DO WITH THE SIX FIGURES YOU SAVED

First off, I would like to say congratulations if you were able
to save six figures. Welcome to America's top 15 percent club.
You have a unique opportunity to truly control your future.
As far as what to do with your six figures, I would definitely
recommend investing it. Personally, I would probably start off
by investing in the stock market if the market is down. I would
sit in a few stable companies and wait for the market to return.
Bear in mind, this may take a few years depending on the state
of the economy. Another option I would consider if I wanted
to play it safe are CDs. You can put your money in for a year
and get back 3 to 4 percent. However, there are better ways to
make your money double. Another option that's a little more
work is e-commerce. You buy goods and sell them at a profit.
There are many websites out there where you can buy items at
a discount and resell them online. Next would be real estate.
Real estate is always a good investment. You just have to figure
out what area works best for you. The last thing would be to
invest in what you feel makes sense. If you were disciplined
enough to save six figures, you should be disciplined enough to
navigate the world of investing. Just take your time and most
importantly do your research.

17. WHAT TO DO WHEN YOU GET OUT

There are several things you should do either before or as soon
as you get out of the service. First thing, if you haven't already,
is to invest in real estate, whether it's buying your first place,

buying a condo and renting it out, getting into Airbnb, or flipping properties. What area you decide to pursue is up to you, but one thing is for certain: you should 100 percent invest in real estate. Real estate is one of the fastest ways to gain and maintain wealth, so go get you a piece of the American pie.

The next thing you should do shortly after you leave the military is pursue your dream. There is no better time than when you're fresh out of service. Whether it's starting your own business, learning a new field, getting your pilot license, composing your first album, starting your YouTube channel, trying out for *American Idol*...whatever that dream is, go pursue it as soon as you get out. If you listened to me during this book, you should have the resources, discipline, and structure to put 100 percent into your dream. Go out and make it happen.

The last advice I have for you is to enjoy the process. Look, life isn't easy. It may be easier for some, but truth be told, it isn't easy for most. You have to find your peace and happiness on your way to the top. If you don't, when you get to the top you'll notice it's the same as the bottom. Remember, money means everything until you have it. Once you have it, it means nothing. It is just another tool in your shed of resources.

LAST BUT NOT LEAST

Find your peace, find your family, find your friends, find your community, find your purpose, and most importantly, find your God. You have to live life to the fullest regardless of your path. Remember, life isn't promised, so live every day to the fullest. I'll leave you with a quote from Dr. Myles Munroe: "Most people die at age 25 and are buried at age 65." By that he means that most people give up on their dreams at twenty-five and go through the motions until physical death. Don't let that be you.

Take the military and use it as a stepping stone to help you build a better life. Find your passion and live it out. Be a light in this dark world. Good luck with your journey! God bless.

APPENDIX

LIST OF MILITARY DISCOUNTS

Note: All discounts are subject to change. The following information is readily available to the public and is only stated to acknowledge the vast amount of discounts available to service members. This list does not include every discount available to military personnel. That list would be a book in itself.

RETAIL

- 5.11 Tactical: Spend $100, get $20 off
- Adidas: 30 percent off regular-price orders
- All American Clothing: 15 percent off
- Allen Edmonds: 15 percent off active-duty
- Alpha Industries:15 percent off
- American Giant: Up to 20 percent off
- Armed Forces Gear: 10 percent off active-duty and retired
- Ariat: 10 percent off
- Baby Tula: 15 percent off

- Bass Pro Shops: 5 percent off
- Bates Footwear: Active and military veterans get 15 percent off
- BN3TH: 20 percent military discount to military veterans
- Bob's Stores: 10 percent off for active-duty and retired military service members
- Bonobos: 20 percent discount
- Brooklyn Bedding: Active and retired US military get 25 percent off.
- Buckle: 10 percent military discount
- Cabela's: Active and retired military get 5 percent discount.
- Carhartt: 25 percent off on select apparel and accessories
- Carter's: Free shipping to all APO and FPO addresses for online orders over $50
- Champion: 10 percent military discount to active-duty and retired US military personnel
- Clarks: 10 percent military discount for veterans, retirees, and active-duty US military personnel
- Cole Haan: 20 percent discount for active-duty, reservists, veterans, and National Guard
- Columbia: 10 percent military discount to service members
- Converse: 15 percent discount for active-duty, reservists, veterans, and National Guard
- Dagne Dover: 20 percent discount to US military service members
- DC Shoes: 5 percent off for veterans, active-duty members, and retirees
- Dickies: 10 percent military discount to active and retired US military personnel
- Dirt Cheap: 10 percent military discount to veterans, reservists, retirees, active-duty service members, and their dependents

- Eastbay: 20 percent discount for active and retired US military personnel and their dependents
- Eight Sleep: 10 percent military discount to active-duty members, veterans, retirees, military spouses, and dependents
- Ergobaby: 20 percent discount to active and veteran US military members
- Fathead: 10 percent military discount to US armed forces members
- Foot Locker: 10 percent discount to active-duty, reserve, and retired military members
- Footaction: 15 percent off for active-duty and retired military personnel
- Gabe's: 10 percent discount to current and former US military and National Guard
- Galen Leather: 8 percent discount to US military members, veterans, and dependents
- GameStop: 10 percent in-store military discount
- GhostBed: 30 percent discount for active-duty, retired military, veterans, and military family members
- Goodwill Southern New England: 20 percent discount for US military service members with a valid ID
- Goodwill Washington: 10 percent discount for US armed forces personnel
- Hanes.com: 10 percent discount to active-duty and retired US military service members
- Heated Clothing 4 U: 15 percent discount on regular-price items to US military personnel
- Home Depot: 10 percent military discount to veterans and active-duty service members
- Huk Gear: Variable discount for active and retired US military members

- HYLETE: 30 percent off for veterans, reservists, and active members
- JackThreads: 15 percent military discount to veterans, active-duty service members, and their spouses
- JOANN: 15 percent off for US armed forces, National Guard, and reserves
- Jockey: 10 percent discount to active-duty, retired military service members, and their families
- Joe Bob Outfitters: 5 percent discount to active and retired members of the US armed forces
- Just My Size: 10 percent online discount to active-duty and retired military service members
- Karen Kane: 20 percent discount on online orders to active-duty, retired military service members, and their families
- Kids Foot Locker: 10 percent off for military personnel
- Layla Sleep: 20 percent off for active, retired, and reserve military members
- Lovesac: 5 percent off select bedding products for US military service members
- Luminary Global: 5 percent discount and free shipping to active-duty, retired military, reservists, veterans, National Guard, and dependents
- Malouf: 35 percent off for active and retired US military service members
- Man Crates: 10 percent off for US military members and their families
- Merrell: 10 percent discount to US military service members, veterans, and their families
- Michaels: 15 percent in-store discount to active-duty and retired service members
- Mountain Khakis: Up to 40 percent military discount for

active-duty personnel, veterans, and military family members

- Murse World: 10 percent military discount to active-duty members, retirees, veterans, and military spouses
- National Tuxedo Rentals: 5 percent off for active, retired, and reserve military members
- New Balance: 10 percent discount to members of the US armed forces
- Newton Running: 20 percent military discount plus free shipping to active-duty service members and their families
- Nike: 10 percent for veterans, retirees, and active-duty service members
- Nitro Circus: 15 percent discount code to all US military members
- Northern Tool: 10 percent military discount to active-duty members and veterans of the US armed forces
- Obscure Belts: 10 percent discount to US military personnel
- Off-Grid Knives: 10 percent off for veterans and active-duty service members
- OGIO: 15 percent military discount to veterans, reservists, retirees, and active-duty members of the US armed forces
- One Hanes Place: 10 percent military discount to current and former members of the US armed forces
- OshKosh B'Gosh: Free shipping on online orders over to all APO and FPO shipping addresses
- Puma: 10 percent off for veterans and active members of the US military
- Quiksilver: 15 percent military discount to US armed forces personnel
- Rack Room Shoes: 10 percent discount to military personnel and their families

- Reebok: 50 percent discount to members of the US armed forces
- ROAD iD: Military discount to active and retired US armed forces members and their family members
- Roxy: 15 percent military discount for US armed forces personnel
- Saddleback Leather: Veterans, active military members, and their dependents receive a discount on Saddleback Leather products.
- Shinola: 15 percent military discount to active-duty personnel and veterans
- Southern Tide: 20 percent discount to active-duty, veterans, and their spouses
- Sperry: 15 percent discount to veterans and active-duty US military members
- Steel Horse Leather: 10 percent off for active and retired US military personnel
- Sword & Plough: 20 percent military discount to US veterans and active-duty personnel
- Tecovas: 20 percent discount to current and former service members
- The North Face:10 percent off for veterans, reservists, and active-duty US armed forces personnel
- Tread Labs: 25 percent off for active-duty military personnel, veterans, and their families
- UF Pro: Free shipping and product discounts for US military personnel
- Under Armour: 20 percent discount on select purchases to active and military personnel and their family members
- Unique Gifts Store: 20 percent discount to veterans, active-duty, and their family members

- UNTUCKit: 25 percent discount to active-duty, veterans, and military family members
- Vera Bradley: 15 percent online discount to members of the US military
- Veterans Nation: 15 percent discount to active military, reservists, veterans, and military dependents
- Vineyard Vines: 15 percent off for veterans and active members
- Wilsons Leather: In-store discounts to active and retired US armed forces personnel and their families
- Wrangler: 10 percent military discount to active members and veterans of the US armed forces
- Yankee Candle: 10 percent discount to active and retired military service members
- YETI Coolers: Online discounts to veterans, active-duty, retired, and reserve members of the US military or National Guard

TRAVEL

- Air Transat: 25 percent off Option Plus if available and 50 percent off excess baggage fees for US military members
- Alaska Airlines: 15 percent off in-flight meals, and up to five free check-in bags for active US armed forces members and their family. Veterans Advantage members also receive an extra 5 percent discount.
- Amtrak: 10 percent off for active-duty military personnel
- Best Price Cruises & Tours: Discounted pricing on select cruise lines for US military personnel
- Carnival Cruise Lines: Discounted rates to active-duty and retired military personnel

- Capitol Corridor: 15 percent off for US military personnel and their immediate family members
- CIE Tours: 5 percent military discount to active-duty members, retirees, and their immediate family members
- Clipper Vacations: 10 percent off select fares for adults and up to 50 percent off the standard adult fare for children of active-duty, reserve, and retired military personnel
- Delta Vacations: Military discounts ranging from $50–$300 on select bookings
- Expedia: 10 percent off of select hotels, exclusive travel deals, and other benefits for active and retired military personnel
- Grand Canyon Railway & Hotel: 15 percent discount on train, hotel, and RV park reservations to active military members and veterans
- Greyhound Bus Lines: 10 percent discount to active-duty military personnel and their families
- Hillsborough Area Regional Transit Authority (HART): Permanent discount to veterans with Veteran Administration Disable ID status "Service Connected"
- iVenture Card: 10 percent off any online purchase of the Unlimited Attractions Pass or Flexi Attractions Pass for US armed forces personnel
- JetBlue: 5 percent discount, special military fares, and support assistance to active-duty and retired service members
- Kingsmill Resort: 15 percent off select nights for military services members
- Lufthansa: 5 percent off select flights for US military personnel
- MSC Cruises: 10 percent off active and retired members of the US military

- Peter Pan Bus Lines: 15 percent off the full adult fare for active-duty and retired military personnel
- Princess Cruises: Veterans, active-duty, retired, and disabled military personnel receive up to $250 on-board spending money from Princess Cruises.
- Riverside Transit Agency (RTA): Active-duty military personnel are eligible for discounted fares.
- Royal Caribbean: Discounted rates for active-duty military, reservists, veterans, and military spouses
- RTD Denver: Free bus and rail fares to active-duty and National Guard
- Silver Airways: 11 percent off select flights for active-duty service members and their spouses
- Southwest Airlines: Discounted ticket to active-duty military personnel and their families
- Sun Metro: Discounted fares for active and retired military personnel and their dependents
- United Airlines: 5 percent off airline tickets plus extra baggage allowance for active-duty, retired service members, and their families
- United Vacations: Up to $300 off bookings for US military service members
- Vacations to Go: Special rates on select cruise lines for active, retired military, reservists, and veterans

AUTOMOTIVE

- Aceable: 50 percent discount on select driving courses for active-duty and retired US military members
- Amanda Products: 10 percent military discount to active-duty service members and veterans

- Ameraguard Truck Accessories: 15 percent discounts to members of the US military
- Anthem Wheels: 15 percent discount to current and former US armed forces
- Audi USA: Military discount savings to active-duty service members
- Auto Accessories Garage: 20 percent discount to active-duty military members and veterans
- AutoMeter: 15 percent off for US military active-duty and veterans including reservists and family members
- Bell Helmets: Pro Deal Program for military service members
- BMW North America: Military discounts to service members deployed stateside or overseas who want to purchase or lease a BMW vehicle. Contact your local dealer.
- CARiD: 10 percent discount to service members
- Chevrolet: Chevy offers a special military discount rate to active-duty and retired military service members and their spouses. Valid ID is required.
- Chrysler: Active and retired service members can get $500 bonus cash when purchasing or leasing select Chrysler models.
- Cycle Gear: 10 percent military discount to active-duty and retired military personnel
- Ford: $500 bonus cash for active and retired members of the armed forces during the purchase or lease of a new vehicle
- General Motors: $500 cash allowance on select Chevrolet, Buick, and GMC vehicles or $1,000 on select Cadillac vehicles for US military personnel who want to lease or purchase a new vehicle
- Harley-Davidson: Free shipping to APO/DPO address, overseas military sale program, discounted motorcycle storage,

and military financing with no down payment for all military service members

- Hyundai: $500 credit when purchasing a new Hyundai vehicle for active-duty, retired military personnel, veterans, and National Guard service members
- Jiffy Lube: 25 percent off for veterans and active-duty military members
- KC HiLITES: 10 percent discount to active-duty service members
- Kia Motors: $400 off on purchase or lease of a new vehicle for active and retired US service personnel and their immediate family
- Morris 4×4: 5 percent military discount to members of the US armed forces and National Guard
- Nissan: $500 cash allowance on vehicle purchases for US service members
- Pep Boys: 10 percent discount for active and retired members of the US military
- TireBuyer: 7 percent discount to active-duty, veterans, and their immediate family members
- Toyota Financial Services: $500 bonus cash to active, retired, and reserve US military personnel
- Urban Helmets: 15 percent discount to veterans and active members of the US military
- Volkswagen: $500 cash bonus when leasing or buying a new Volkswagen vehicle
- Volvo: $1,000 purchase bonus or $500 lease bonus to US military personnel. Free shipping, maintenance, and roadside assistance services for service members deployed overseas.

CAR RENTAL

- Alamo Car Rental: Rental discounts plus perks for active, retired and veterans of the armed forces
- Avis Car Rental: 25 percent off for active, retired, and veterans of the US armed forces
- Budget Car Rental: 25 percent discount to US duty, veterans, and National Guard members
- Budget Truck Rental: 20 percent off for active-duty and retired military service members
- Dollar Car Rental: 5 percent discount on retail rates plus additional benefits
- Enterprise Car Rental: 5 percent discounts to current and former members of the US service members
- Hertz Car Rental: $5/day per vehicle discounted rate, free upgrades, and free Hertz Gold Plus Rewards membership to active-duty and veterans
- National Car Rental: Special rates, discounts, and other benefits for US service members
- Penske Truck Rental: 10 percent rental discount to active-duty and veteran US armed forces members
- Rental Cover: 30 percent discount to active military personnel
- Sixt: 5 percent off car rentals plus other benefits
- Thrifty: 5 percent military discount to US veterans and free advantage members

SPORTS

- Atlanta Hawks: Discounts on regular-season tickets to US armed forces members
- Baltimore Orioles: 20 percent off games for active, retired, and reserve military members

- Baltimore Ravens: Reduced prices on select game tickets to active-duty service members
- Callaway Golf: 15 percent discount on golf equipment and accessories to US veterans
- Champs Sports: 15 percent off for active-duty and retired military service members
- Chicago Bulls: Discounts on game tickets on Veterans Day
- Chubbies Shorts: 10 percent discount on select apparel to members of the US armed forces
- Cleveland Guardians: 20 percent discount on game tickets for active-duty and retired military service members
- Fanatics: 15 percent off at Fanatics.com for active-duty, National Guard, veterans, and military family members
- Leisure Pro: 6 percent military discount to active-duty and retired US armed forces members and their spouses and dependents
- Lund Boats: $100 to $1,500 off on select models to members of the US armed forces
- Martinsville Speedway: Discounts on select tickets to active-duty US armed forces members
- Military Tee Times:15 percent discount on select golf courses to US military veterans
- Minnesota Timberwolves: Active and retired military members receive a 30 percent discount on Minnesota Timberwolves game tickets
- MLB Shop: 15 percent discount to US military personnel and their family members
- Moosejaw: 20 percent military discount on full-priced items to former and current members of the US armed forces
- NASCAR Racing Experience: 10 percent off retail products
- NASCAR Shop: 10 percent discount to military service members and their families

- NBA Store: 15 percent military discount to active-duty and retired members of the US armed forces
- NFL Shop: 15 percent off online orders plus free shipping for former and active military service members
- NHL Shop: 15 percent off online orders to active-duty and retired military personnel, their spouses, and dependents
- Orlando Magic: Discounts on select game tickets to active military, veterans, reservists, retirees, and military dependents
- Patriots Pro Shop: 10 percent discount to US military service members
- Phoenix Suns: 20 percent off Phoenix Suns home game tickets
- Pittsburgh Pirates: Military discounts on home game tickets to US armed forces members and their families
- Pocono Raceway: Ticket discounts to active-duty and retired military personnel and their families
- Portland Trail Blazers: Discounts on select games for active-duty military, veterans, reservists, and military dependents
- Profox Racing: 10 percent off regular-price items for current and former service members of the US military
- PXG: Active and retired US military personnel can apply to the PXG for Heroes program to get discounts, which saves money on select items.
- San Antonio Spurs: 40 percent off game tickets for veterans and active-duty members of the US armed forces
- St. Louis Cardinals: One free ticket on select games in addition to a $2 discount on the admission fee to the Cardinals Hall of Fame Museum
- Talladega Superspeedway: Discounted tickets to military members and their families

- Tampa Bay Rays: Discounts on select game tickets to active-duty, retired military, and veterans
- TaylorMade Golf: 15 percent discount for active and retired military service members and their spouses and dependents
- Texas Motor Speedway: Active-duty military, retirees, and veterans can get two discounted tickets on select races.
- Washington Nationals: 30 percent discount on home games for active and retired military members
- Washington Wizards: 20 percent discount on home game tickets to active, reserve, and retired members of the US armed forces

TECHNOLOGY

- 23andMe: Military service members and veterans can get a 10 percent discount plus other benefits.
- Apple: 10 percent off for active-duty members and veterans of the US military
- AT&T: 25 percent off each AT&T Unlimited wireless line plus special monthly rates
- C Spire: 10 percent off select wireless plans
- Cobra Electronics: 20 percent online discount to active, retired, veterans, and military family members
- Cove Security: Exclusive discount to members of the US military
- Dell: 10 percent discount to military service members and their families
- DISH Outdoors: Veterans and active-duty military members receive a discount on DISH Outdoors Satellite Antenna Bundle
- ESET: 25 percent military discount on all home antivirus products

- Games to Grunts: Active-duty military and veterans are eligible for special discounts on hundreds of digital games.
- Guardline: 10 percent discount to US military personnel, veterans, and their immediate family members
- HELM Audio: 50 percent discount for US military members on specific items
- iRobot: 20 percent off select iRobot products and free delivery on all robot orders
- Lenovo: 7 percent discount on select products to active military, reservists, veterans, and immediate family members
- Lifelock: 25 percent off membership for US service members
- Malwarebytes: 20 percent off for veterans, active-duty service members, and their family
- Microsoft: 10 percent discount on select products to active and retired military personnel and their families
- Miku: 20 percent for active, retired, and reserve members of the military including veterans, spouses, and dependents
- Motorola: 10 percent discount to active-duty military, reservists, retirees, and veterans
- My Alarm Center: $150 cash credit to current and veteran members of the US military
- PC Richard & Son: Military discounts to veterans and active-duty members
- Ring: 20 percent off for veterans, active-duty US military members, and their dependents
- Samsung: 30 percent to members of the US armed forces
- Sennheiser: 20 percent military discount to members of the US armed forces
- Silk Smartish: 15 percent military discount on select phones and accessories to US armed forces members
- Sprint: Active and retired military service members can save up to 50 percent on Sprint Unlimited lines

- Targus: 25 percent discount to veterans, reservists, military dependents, and active-duty members of the US military
- T-Mobile: T-Mobile offers discounts to veterans, active-duty military members, and their families.
- TravlFi: Veterans and active duty military members can get $40 off purchase.
- US Cellular: 15 percent discount on monthly calling plan charges for active-duty, reserve, and retired military service members
- Verizon: Verizon offers military discounts on select wireless plans to active-duty US military members, veterans, and military families.
- Vimeo: 10 percent off annual subscriptions
- VirtualPBX: 20 percent discount to active-duty and retired military service members

FIREARMS

- Aero Precision: Active-duty military members and veterans can get 10 percent off.
- Blue Force Gear: Military discount on accessories
- Bud's Gun Shop: Discounts on select firearms and accessories to active and retired members of the US armed forces and National Guard
- Centennial Gun Club: Active and reserve members of the US military can get $50 off the registration fee and 20 percent off monthly dues.
- CVA Firearms: 20 percent military discount on select products to US armed forces members who can provide valid proof of military service
- Daniel Defense: US military veterans, retirees, and active members can apply for a firearm discount at Daniel Defense.

- FN America: Active and retired US military personnel can get a discount on one firearm per category per year (pistol, shotgun, carbine) at authorized FN dealers or distributors.
- Geissele Automatics: Active-duty military members can get 10 percent off when they sign up using their valid military address.
- Glock: Firearm discounts to active and retired US military personnel through their Blue Label Program
- Lancer Systems: Special pricing on firearm components to veterans and active-duty military members
- Lehigh Defense: Active and retired US armed forces members are eligible for a 10 percent military discount
- Lockhart Tactical: Minimum 10 percent military discount to veterans and active-duty US armed forces members when they use the code MIL10POL. For larger discounts of up to 60 percent, sign up for their Honor Program for free by using your valid military ID.
- Nightforce Optics: Individual and agency discounts to active and reserve members of the US military
- POF USA: Military discounts on select products to active-duty US armed forces members with valid ID
- Precision Bluing: Active and retired military members can get 10 percent off services.
- Prepper Gun Shop: All active-duty and retired members of the US military and National Guard can receive discounted pricing on select products.
- Primary Arms: 10 percent discount on select brands to active-duty military personnel and veterans
- Rainier Arms: Active-duty military personnel are eligible for special pricing.
- Rick Hinderer Knives: 10 percent discount on XM-18 products plus priority orders for active members of the US military

- Ruger: Active, reserve, and retired members of the military are eligible for discounts on select firearms.
- Shooter's Pro Shop: 10 percent discount to US armed forces personnel
- Sig Sauer: Active and retired military personnel can qualify for discounts on select products when they register for Sig Sauer's Armed Professionals Program.
- SilencerCo: Military discounts to active service members and veterans when they sign up for the SPEQ Program
- Springfield Armory: Discounts to active-duty military, retirees, and National Guard members
- Steiner Scopes: Active, reserve, and retired military personnel can apply for discounts on select products.
- Stcyr: Discount on select firearms to active, reserve, and retired military personnel, including National Guard
- Sticky Holsters: 15 percent military discount to veterans and active-duty US armed forces members
- Stun & Run Self Defense: Extra 10 percent discount to active military members, reservists, veterans, retirees, and military dependents
- Surefire: Active and reserve members of the military and National Guard can get 20 percent off products (except batteries).
- Tactical Gear: 10 percent discount to active-duty military, veterans, and their families when you sign in with a valid Troop ID account.
- US Optics: Active, reserve, and retired military service members can apply to the discount program to receive exclusive discounts.
- Volquartsen Firearms: 10 percent military discount to active-duty US armed forces personnel
- Vortex Optics: Active and retired US military personnel can

save up to 40 percent on riflescopes, red-dot sights, and other tactical accessories.

- Wolverine Supplies: 10 percent discount on regular-priced products to US armed forces personnel

JEWELRY

- 1776 Mint: Free shipping on all copper and silver figurine orders to US military members
- Alpine Rings: US military members, veterans, and their families can save 10 percent on jewelry purchases year-round
- Antique Jewelry Mall: Active-duty military members and veterans can get 10 percent off their order.
- Arthur's Jewelers: 10 percent military discount to active-duty and retired US armed forces members
- Blue Nile: Free shipping on all jewelry orders sent to APO, FPO, and DPO addresses
- Elemental Rings: US military members can get 20 percent off men's wedding bands and engagement rings.
- E.M. Smith Jewelers: 10 percent discount on jewelry purchases by US military personnel, in addition to free replacements for watch batteries
- Global Rings Jewelry: Military discounts to active-duty, reserve, and retired members of the US armed forces and National Guard
- Helzberg Diamonds: 10 percent military discount to active-duty and retired US armed forces members and their dependents
- James Free Jewelers: Active and retired US armed forces members and their families can get 15 percent off.
- Larson Jewelers: Active-duty military personnel can get 5 percent off select jewelry orders.

- Lat & Lo: 15 percent military discount on jewelry purchases by US armed forces members who can confirm their military status through VerifyPass
- Malak Jewelers: Current and former US military members can download and print gift certificates.
- Milan on 47th: Active and retired members of the US armed forces can apply for a military discount.
- Moissanite Bridal: 5 percent military discount on select engagement rings to active-duty US armed forces members
- QALO: Military discount to current and former members of the US armed forces and their spouses and dependents
- Robbins Brothers: US military members and their families can get up to $400 off select engagement rings.
- Roger & Hollands: 10 percent discount on single jewelry orders by veterans, retirees, reservists, and active members of the US military
- Serendipity Diamonds: US armed forces personnel can get a 20 percent military discount.
- Since1910: 10 percent discount on select engagement rings to US military personnel
- Steven Singers Jewelers: 5 percent military discount to members of the US armed forces
- The Pearl Source: 10 percent military discount to active and retired US armed forces members and their registered dependents
- Tiffany & Co.: 10 percent off wedding bands and engagement rings to active-duty members, reservists, and veterans of the US military
- Wedding Rings Depot: Veterans and active-duty US military personnel can get 10 percent off their order.
- White Flash: 1 percent military discount on engagement rings to active-duty service members

- Wonder Jewelers: 15 percent discount on diamond jewelry to members of the US military, and free FedEx priority shipping to US postal addresses and APO/FPO addresses

ENTERTAINMENT

- A Story before Bed: Military personnel deployed overseas can access 250,000 free recordings of bedtime stories for their children.
- AMC Movie Theatres: Participating theaters offer military discounts to active-duty and retired US armed forces personnel.
- Angelika Film Center: Active-duty military members who can show their valid ID to the box office can pay only $11.50 for tickets and also receive free popcorn every Wednesday.
- Atlanta Rocks Indoor Climbing: Active-duty military members receive 10 percent off the regular climbing fee.
- Cracked It! Escape Games: US armed forces members can get a 10 percent discount on Escape Rooms and other Cracked It! Escape Games.
- Crayola Experience: The Crayola Experience in Orlando offers a $3 general admission discount to military members.
- Fender Play: 30 percent discount on their Annual Plan to active, retired, and reserve US armed forces personnel and their immediate family members
- Ford's Theatre: Active-duty and veteran members of the US military can save up to 50 percent on select tickets.
- Houston Ballet: 25 percent discount on select shows to active and retired members of the US military and National Guard and their spouses and dependents
- Marcus Theatres: Active and retired members of the US

military are eligible for special pricing of $7.50 at participating locations.

- Musician's Friend: 10 percent discount on a single item worth $199 or more to active and retired members of the US military
- OTL Seat Filler Club: US armed forces members can join the club for a discounted price in order to gain free access to local music and entertainment events.
- Showcase Cinemas: Active-duty military personnel and their dependents are qualified for a special $7.50 admission price at all locations except Showcase Superlux in Chestnut Hill, Massachusctts.
- Sky Zone Trampoline Park: Ticket discounts to US military personnel and their families
- SiriusXM Radio: 25 percent subscription discount to active-duty members, reservists, and veterans of the US armed forces along with military spouses and dependents
- Stratz Center: Special ticket prices on select shows to military personnel with valid ID
- Ticket Club: Active-duty military members and veterans can apply for free
- Veteran Ticket Foundation: Exclusive and discounted tickets for all kinds of different events to active-duty service members, veterans, and their military dependents

HEALTH AND FITNESS

- 5 Star Nutrition: 5 percent military discount to active and retired US armed forces members
- 24 Hour Fitness: Active and reserve US military personnel can apply for a free three-day gym pass. They are also eligi-

ble for $5 monthly fees with no initial payment when they sign up for select basic gym memberships.

- Atera Spas: US armed forces members with service ID are eligible for military discounts at participating locations.
- Atkins: 15 percent military discount on select fitness bars and shakes to veterans and active-duty US armed forces members
- Beachbody: Active-duty military, retirees, and veterans are eligible for a 25 percent discount.
- Best Price Nutrition: 5 percent discount on supplements to US military members
- Bodybuilding.com: US armed forces members can get a 10 percent military discount.
- Capital City Gymnastics, South Carolina: 10 percent discount to US military members and their families
- C4 HealthLabs: Veterans, active-duty members, and military dependents can get a 20 percent discount on CBD oil.
- CVS Pharmacy: 20 percent military discount on every order plus free shipping to Veterans Advantage members
- Dragonfly Hot Yoga: Veterans and active-duty US armed forces members can buy a ten-class pass for $150.
- DrOwl: Free and secure way for VA members to access, understand, and share their VA medical records
- Empower Pharmacy: 25 percent discount on compounded medications to active, retired, disabled, and veteran members of the US military
- Fitness 4 Home Superstore: Discounts to US military veterans, reservists, active-duty personnel, and their dependents
- Gold's Gym: Discounted membership and monthly fees to veterans and active-duty military personnel
- Cal Banyan's Hypnosis.org: 20 percent military discount on select training courses to active-duty members and veterans of the US armed forces

- Kayla Itsines: 20 percent discount to US military personnel
- Lazarus Naturals: Veterans can get 60 percent off their purchase.
- Massage Envy: Military discount program offers up to $60 in savings a year for all active-duty US armed forces members.
- Onnit: 15 percent discount to active-duty US military members
- Pure Formulas: 10 percent military discount to former and current members of the US armed forces and their spouses and dependents
- Qardio: US veterans, active-duty military members, and retirees can get 20 percent off devices.
- REDCON1: 25 percent military discount to active-duty members and veterans of the US armed forces
- Rep Fitness: Active and retired US armed forces members can get 5 percent off select exercise equipment.
- SmartStyle Hair Salon: 10 percent military discount on products and services to active-duty, retired, and veteran service members
- Tommie Copper: 15 percent military discount to active and retired US armed forces members
- UFC Gym: US military members can get a free thirty-day gym pass at select gyms that participate in the Harley-Davidson Military Program.
- Weight Crafters: Active-duty members, reservists, and veterans of the US armed forces can apply for discounts.
- WellnessMats: 25 percent military discount to active and retired members of the US armed forces
- YMCA: Active-duty service members, reservists, and their families can apply for the YMCA Military Outreach Program and child respite services at participating locations.

HOTELS AND RESORTS

- Altoona Grand Hotel, Pennsylvania: Members of the US military with valid ID can get 15 percent off select rooms.
- Atlantis Casino Resort & Spa: 15 percent discount to active and retired military members and their families
- Atlantis Paradise Island: US military members can save 25 percent on hotel rates in addition to free unlimited access to the water park and casino in the Bahamas.
- Bally's Hotel & Casino: Atlantic City and Las Vegas locations offer a 35 percent military discount to US armed forces members and veterans.
- Beaches Resorts: Active-duty members of the US military can get a 10 percent discount.
- Beachwoods Resort: US military members with valid ID can get 15 percent off select bookings.
- Best Western Hotels & Resort: Military discounts to active-duty and retired service members
- Castle Resorts & Hotels: US military personnel and their family members can get discounted rates on select resorts and hotels in Hawaii.
- Caesars Hotel & Casino: US military members and veterans can get a 35 percent discount in Las Vegas and Atlantic City.
- Cheeca Lodge & Spa, Florida: 10 percent room discount to active and retired military members
- Choice Hotels: Discounts on select room rates to active-duty and retired military personnel
- Country Inns & Suites: Active and retired military members, as well as their spouses, are eligible for discounts at participating hotels as part of their Military 1st Program.
- Cromwell Hotel, Las Vegas: 35 percent military discount to active and retired US armed forces members

- Dreams Resorts and Spas: US military members are eligible for a 10 percent discount on booking fees.
- Embassy Suites by Hilton: Special rates and exclusive benefits to US military personnel and their families
- Extended Stay America: US military personnel are eligible for exclusive discounts and services on select rooms and suites.
- Flamingo Hotel & Casino, Las Vegas: Veterans and active-duty members of the US armed forces can get 10 percent off select rooms and suites.
- Foxwoods Resort & Casino: 15 percent military discount on hotel rooms and $5 off scooter rentals to active and retired US armed forces members
- Grande Shores Ocean Resort: Active-duty, retired, and reserve members of the US military can get a discount on select rooms.
- Great Wolf Lodge: 30 percent Howlin' Heroes Discount to active and retired US military personnel
- Hampton Inn & Suites: Exclusive room rates and benefits to US armed forces members
- Harrah's Hotel & Casino: US military members can get a 10 percent discount.
- Hawk's Cay Resort, Florida Keys: Active members and veterans of the US armed forces can get 15 percent off their stay.
- Hilton Hotel & Resorts: Hilton offers a 10 percent discount on hotel and resort room rates to US military members and their families.
- Horseshoe Hotel & Casino: Veterans and active-duty members of the US armed forces can get a 10 percent military discount at select locations.
- Hotwire: 10 percent military discount on hotel bookings of $100 and above

- Howard Johnson Hotels: Active-duty military personnel are eligible for special rates and other benefits at participating hotels.
- InterContinental Hotel Group: Current and former US armed forces personnel are eligible for discounts at participating hotels.
- La Quinta Inns & Suites: Active-duty service members, veterans, and military spouses can get 12 percent off room rates.
- Lake Powell Resorts & Marinas, Defiance House Lodge: 10 percent military discount on lodging to active-duty members and veterans
- Marriott Hotels & Resorts: Active-duty US military personnel are eligible for discounted room rates based on availability.
- Mermaid Cottages: Active and retired US armed forces members can get a 5 percent military discount.
- Mesa Verde National Park, Colorado:10 percent discount on select Far View Lodge room rates to veterans and active-duty military members
- MGM Resorts: Former and current members of the US military and National Guard can get discounts on select rooms and services.
- Motel 6: 10 percent discount to retired and active US military members
- Nobu Hotel, Las Vegas: US armed forces members and veterans get a 10 percent military discount.
- OYO Hotel and Casino, Las Vegas: 15 percent discount to US military members
- Palms Casino Resort: 15 percent military discount to active-duty members, veterans, and their families
- Paris Las Vegas Hotel & Casino: US armed forces members and veterans can get a 10 percent military discount on select rooms.

- Pinehurst Resort: Active and retired US military personnel will receive a 10 percent discount on select activities, accommodations, and spa packages.
- Planet Hollywood Resort & Casino, Las Vegas: US armed forces members who can sign in with Troop ID to verify their military status can get 10 percent off select rooms.
- Rainier Lodging: Members of the US military can get 10 percent off room rates at Three Bears Cabins.
- Red Lion Hotels: Active or retired US military personnel can get 15 percent off their stay at participating hotels.
- Red Roof Inn: 15 percent discount to active-duty and retired military service members
- Rio All-Suite Hotel & Casino, Las Vegas: Active and retired US military members can save up to 35 percent on select rooms.
- Sandals Resorts: 10 percent year-round discount to active and retired US military members and their spouses
- Secrets Resorts & Spas: US military personnel can get 10 percent off the best available rate when they book a reservation.
- Seminole Hard Rock Hotel & Casino, Hollywood: Active and retired military members can get 10 percent off.
- The LINQ Hotel & Casino, Las Vegas: US military personnel can get 35 percent off room rates.
- Turf Valley: 25 percent military discount on one lunch or dinner entrée and an option for late check-out at 6:00 p.m. to US military guests at Alexandra's American Fusion
- Village Realty, Outer Banks, North Carolina: Military discount of up to 5 percent on select vacation rentals
- Wyndham Hotel Group: Discounted rates at participating hotels to active-duty military members

MUSEUMS AND PARKS

- 9/11 Memorial & Museum, Manhattan, New York: Free admission to active and retired military personnel
- Aquarium of the Pacific, Long Beach, California: US armed forces members and veterans with valid ID can get $3 off adult tickets and $1.50 off child tickets.
- Art Institute of Chicago: Free admission to US military members and their families from Memorial Day through Labor Day
- Boston Children's Museum: Veterans and active-duty US military personnel are eligible for free admission.
- Busch Gardens Theme Park, Tampa, Florida: One free admission per year to active and reserve military members through the Waves of Honor Program
- Busch Gardens Theme Park, Williamsburg, Virginia: Discounts and benefits to US military veterans and active-duty members through the Waves of Honor Program
- Butchart Gardens, Victoria, Canada: 50 percent admission fee to US military members
- Carnegie Science Center: Active-duty military and veterans with service IDs can get 50 percent off admission rates.
- Dallas Zoo: $2 discount on admission fees to US military members
- Denver Art Museum: Members of the US armed forces are eligible for general admission discounts.
- Diggerland Construction Amusement Park, New Jersey: Discounted tickets to active military personnel and up to three family members
- Dollywood Parks & Resorts: 30 percent military discount on single-day tickets to US armed forces members, including an option to upgrade to a season pass at a reduced price
- Field Museum in Chicago: Active-duty US armed forces

personnel with valid military ID are eligible for free basic admission.

- Flying Squirrel Trampoline Park, Spokane Valley, Washington: US military members and their families can get 50 percent off jump time.
- Houston Zoo: 50 percent discount on general admission tickets for veterans and active members of the US military and their families
- Jungle Island, Miami, Florida: 50 percent discount to active military and a 15 percent discount to veterans and military families
- Kennedy Space Center: Active-duty US military members can get discounted admission fees,
- Kings Dominion: Discounts on single-day admission tickets and Gold Season Passes to military members
- Knott's Berry Farm: US armed forces personnel can get free admission.
- LEGOLAND California Resort: 10 percent military discount and free breakfast per stay on select hotel rooms
- LEGOLAND Florida: Active US military members can get discounted admission fees and vacation packages.
- Milwaukee Public Museum: US armed forces members who visit can receive $4 off admission passes and $1 off the Dome Theater.
- Moody Gardens Hotel, Galveston, Texas: Active-duty US military personnel can get discounted rates.
- Mote Aquarium, Sarasota, Florida: One free admission to active-duty US military members and dependents any day of the week
- Mount Vernon: Free admission to recipients of the Purple Heart medal. Veterans and active-duty military personnel can get $6 off the Grounds Pass.
- New England Aquarium: $10 discount to active-duty mili-

tary members and adult dependents, a $5 discount for child dependents, and a $2 discount to veterans

- Orlando Museum of Art: Veterans and active members of the US military receive free admission.
- Perot Museum of Nature and Science: Free admission to active-duty military members and veterans. Military spouses and dependents receive a $3 discount.
- SeaWorld Orlando: One free admission per year for active-duty military personnel and up to three direct dependents. Veterans and up to three guests can get a 50 percent pricing discount on a single-day ticket.
- SeaWorld San Antonio: Active-duty military members and up to three direct dependents receive one free admission per year. Veterans can get 50 percent off single-day admission tickets for themselves and up to three guests.
- SeaWorld San Diego: One complimentary admission per year to active-duty military members and their families
- Sesame Place, Philadelphia, Pennsylvania: One free ticket per year to active-duty service members and free single-day admission for up to three dependents. Veterans can save 50 percent on single-day tickets for up to six guests.
- Shades of Green: Military discounts of up to 12 percent for tickets to Walt Disney World, Universal Orlando, SeaWorld Orlando, LEGOLAND Orlando, Kennedy Space Center, Busch Gardens Tampa, and more
- Shedd Aquarium: Active-duty military members with a valid ID can get free admission.
- Six Flags Great America: 20 percent discount on a one-day general admission ticket for military personnel. Six Flags over Texas also offers military discounts.
- Space Center Houston: Active-duty military members can get $5 off the general admission fee.

- Universal Orlando Resort: Discounts on select tickets to US armed forces members
- USGS Store: Free "America the Beautiful—National Parks & Federal Recreational Lands" Annual Pass to current US military personnel
- USS Midway Museum, San Diego, California: Free admission to active and reserve US military members
- Walt Disney World Resort: Special promotional tickets with Park Hopper options to members of the US military and National Guard
- Worlds of Fun and Oceans of Fun, Kansas: Military discount to active-duty members and their families
- Yogi Bear's Jellystone Park: Active-duty and retired military personnel with valid ID are eligible for discounts of 10–20 percent at select camping grounds.

FOOD AND RESTAURANT

- 99 Restaurant & Pub: 10 percent military discount to members of Veterans Advantage
- Bonefish Grill: Active and retired US military members can get 10 percent off their order.
- Cicis Pizza: Members of the US military can get discounts at participating outlets.
- El Pollo Loco: 15 percent military discount to US armed forces members
- Golden Corral Buffet & Grill: Current and former members of the US military are eligible for one free dinner at participating branches as part of their Military Appreciation Night.
- Home Chef: US military personnel can get 50 percent off their first order and 10 percent off every subsequent order.

- Joe's Barbecue Company, Alvin, Texas: Veterans can get 10 percent off the breakfast buffet.
- Medieval Times: Discounted ticket prices to current and former US military members
- Noodles & Company: 15 percent discount to customers who are veterans or active members of the US armed forces
- Omaha Steaks: 10 percent discount to active-duty members, retirees, and veterans of the US military and their spouses and dependents
- Outback Steakhouse: Veterans and active-duty US military members can get 10 percent off their entire order every day.
- Ponderosa Steakhouse: 15 percent discount to veterans and active-duty members of the military or National Guard
- Red Robin: US armed forces members can receive special offers when they sign up for their loyalty rewards program.
- Texas de Brazil: Veterans and active-duty military members can get a 20 percent Heroes' Discount.
- Texas Steakhouse: Active and retired members of the US armed forces get a 10 percent military discount.
- Wendy's: Discounts to military personnel with Veterans Advantage membership

FRESH GOODS

- Cheryl's Cookies: Free shipping for all orders delivered to APO and FPO addresses
- Coffee for Less: 10 percent online discount to active and retired military members, veterans, and military spouses
- Costco: Veterans, active-duty military members, and their families can get a $20 Costco Shop Card when they sign up for a new membership.

- DeCicco Family Market: Veterans of the US military are eligible for discounts at participating stores.
- Enfamil: US armed forces personnel can get a 10 percent military discount on select products.
- Gift Basket Bounty: Special care packages for delivery to military addresses. oOverseas shipping of $9.95 applies per gift.
- Greensbury: Military discount on their organic meat and seafood products
- Harry & David: 15 percent discount to military members and veterans. Dependents of Veterans Advantage members can get 15 percent off their order.
- Hickory Farms: Free shipping on military gift baskets to all APO and FPO addresses
- New Seasons Market: Active-duty military members and veterans can get 10 percent off select items every Tuesday.
- Old Time Candy: Free shipping to all APO and FPO addresses
- Thrive Market: Veterans of the US military can sign up for a free membership to get a special discount on their first order, free shipping, and 25–50 percent off retail prices.

PHOTOGRAPHY

- JCPenney Portraits: Free coupon to military service personnel, including a free eight-by-ten standard print, free session fees, a $99.99 digital album, and a 50 percent discount on additional purchases
- Precision Camera & Video, Austin, Texas: Military service members with valid IDs can get 10 percent off photography classes.

VISION

- AC Lens: Active and retired military personnel get 10 percent off select eyewear products.
- AFEyewear: 5 percent discount on select prescription eyeglasses to US military members
- Contacts Direct: 15 percent military discount plus free shipping to US armed forces members
- Coolframes: Active and retired military members and their families can get 5 percent off their order.
- Eyemart Express: 20 percent discount to active-duty and retired military, veterans, and their dependents
- Eyeweb: Veterans and active US military members can get a discount on eyeglasses and safety eyewear.
- Gatorz Eyewear: Veterans and active military personnel can get a military discount code.
- Glasses.com: US military members can get a discount on their purchase when they sign in and verify.
- Kaiser Permanente Eye Care: US armed forces members, veterans, and dependents can get 20 percent off prescription glasses at select optical shops.
- Lasik Plus: Active-duty military personnel and veterans are eligible for a 20 percent discount on eye treatment services.
- Oakley Standard Issue: Reduced pricing to active and retired military service members
- Outlaw Eyewear: Active and retired members of the US military and their spouses can get 25 percent off sunglasses.
- Revision: 30 percent discount on select headgear and eyewear to all members of the US military and their spouses and dependents
- SmartBuyGlasses USA: Military members can get a 10 percent discount on select orders.

- Spy Optic Standard Issue: Exclusive pricing on select eyewear for members of the US military
- SSPEyewear: 15 percent military discount on all purchases by members of the US armed forces
- Sunglass Hut: 15 percent discount to active-duty and retired military, veterans, and military family members

BANKING AND INSURANCE

- America First Credit Union: $100 reward to US military personnel who apply for a savings account, checking account, and credit card services
- American Family Insurance: AMF's Military Business Resource Group provides opportunities and benefits to active-duty service members and veterans of the US armed forces.
- Channeling Stocks:50 percent discount to veterans and active US military members
- Chase: Current and former US military members who open a Chase Premier Plus checking account can qualify for no monthly fees, no minimum balance requirement, and other benefits.
- CSE Insurance Group: Discounted insurance fees to active-duty military members, veterans, and military spouses
- GEICO: 15 percent off annual insurance to active-duty and retired members of the US military and National Guard
- Jackson Hewitt: Special tax considerations to active-duty members of the US armed forces
- Navy Federal Credit Union: US military service personnel, including veterans and Delayed Entry Program members, can get exclusive benefits and discounts when applying for an NFCU savings account.

- PNC Bank: Special rewards, benefits, and loan options to clients who are active or retired members of the US armed forces
- TaxSlayer: No service fee on federal tax return services for active-duty military members
- TurboTax: Military members of ranks E-1–E-5 receive free services for Free and Deluxe editions, and $5 off other products. Ranks E-6 and above receive $5 off all TurboTax federal products.
- US Bank: Does not require monthly maintenance fees and minimum balance for current and former members of the US military when they open a personal checking account
- Watermark Title Agency, Minneapolis, Minnesota: Veterans and active US military members can get discounts through a partnership with Homes for Heroes.

HOUSING AND HOME RENOVATION

- All-American Home Services, Tampa, Florida: US military members can get 10 percent off HVAC installation, maintenance, and repairs.
- Armor Concepts: 25 percent discount on home security products to veterans and active-duty military members
- Bassett Furniture: Veterans, reservists, and active-duty military members can get 30 percent off furniture orders and 10 percent off home accessories.
- Bear Mattress: 25 percent discount to active military, veterans, and their family members
- BelTile: US military members can get a 5 percent discount on stone and tile products.
- Concrete Rockland, Rockland County, New York: 10 percent military discount on home improvement services
- DEKOR Lighting: Current and former US military personnel are eligible for a 10 percent online discount.

- Direct Energy: Members of the US military can get special rates on select plans and services.
- E-Z UP Instant Shelter: Current and former US armed forces members can get a 30 percent military discount.
- GelPro: 25 percent military discount to active-duty and retired US armed forces members, veterans, and military family members
- Heroes San Diego: Veterans, reservists, and active-duty military members can subscribe to earn rebates when they purchase a home.
- Homes for Heroes: Exclusive savings on new home purchases as well as refinancing options to veterans, reservists, and active members of the US military
- Husqvarna: Active-duty members, reservists, and veterans of the US armed forces can get a 10 percent military discount on select lawn products.
- Jacksonville Tile Pro: Veterans and active US military personnel can get 15 percent off tile installation services.
- Kirkland's: 10 percent military discount to active and retired US armed forces members
- Madison Drywallers, Madison, Wisconsin: Veterans and active military members can get 10 percent off all services.
- McCoy's Building Supply: 10 percent year-round discount to eligible active military and veterans, plus extended discounts on Memorial Day and Veterans Day
- Overstock.com: Free Club O Gold membership to active-duty military service members and veterans
- Project Evergreen: Free lawn and landscape services through their GreenCare program and free snow and ice removal services through their SnowCare Program to families of active-duty US military personnel

- Purple: Active, reserve, and retired US military members and their spouses can get 10 percent off select mattresses.
- Sam's Club: $10 gift card to active and retired US military members
- Sherwin-Williams: Active, reserve, and retired US military members and military spouses can get a 15 percent discount on painting supplies.
- Simpli Home: US military members, veterans, and their dependents can get 15 percent off their purchase.
- The Bond Team at RSVP, Washington: Active-duty military members and veterans can get up to 20 percent off real estate services.
- Toolbarn: 5 percent military discount on select items to veterans, retirees, and active-duty members of the US military or National Guard
- Tucson Wood Refinishing: 10 percent discount to active and retired members of the armed services
- US Bank: Veterans Advantage members are eligible for discounts on home loans and refinancing options.
- VOLT Lighting: Active members and veterans of the US military and their families can get a 10 percent discount.
- Worx: 10 percent discount on tools and home supplies to active-duty military members and veterans

PETS

- American Airlines Cargo: 50 percent military discount on pet transport fees
- Best Bully Sticks: Active US military members can get 15 percent off their online purchase.
- Happy Tails Travel: Exclusive discounts on pet relocation services to all active-duty military, veterans, and military spouses

- Pet Air Carrier, LLC: Military families receive a discount of $125 (international flight) or $50 (domestic flight) for the first pet and a $25 discount for each additional pet.
- Pet Palace: 10 percent military discount on pet bath and boarding fees to active-duty members of the US military
- Pets for Patriots: Current or retired US military members including veterans are eligible for a 10 percent discount on pet care services plus other benefits on pet adoption and training.
- Pet Supermarket: US military personnel can get 10 percent off on the last Tuesday of every month.
- Tri-County Humane Society: Veterans and active members of the US military do not need to pay adoption fees for cats who are six months old and older.
- United Airlines: Special pet transportation benefits to active-duty military personnel and their spouses who are traveling on official duty

LEGAL

- Apex Legal Services: Discounts on select legal services to veterans of the US military
- LaBovick & Diaz Law Group: 15 percent off monetary attorney fees for the legal cases of active-duty military members and veterans
- LegalDocsA2Z: Military discounts of up to 15 percent on select legal services to active-duty service members

OUTDOORS

- Attitash Mountain Resort: Discount on lift tickets for active and retired US military members

- Big 5 Sporting Goods: 10 percent discount to active-duty, reserve, retired, and veteran members of the US military
- Brickwood Ovens: Special pricing to active military personnel
- Cody KOA, Wyoming: 15 percent military discount to members of the US armed forces and National Guard
- Cranmore Mountain Resort: $15 discount on lift tickets to active military members and their dependents. Retirees can get the $15 discount for themselves only
- Crossbow Nation: Active and retired military personnel can get 10 percent off Scorpyd crossbows.
- Gerber Gear: Current and former members of the US armed forces, reserves, and National Guard can apply to Gerber Gear's Pro Program to receive exclusive offers and discounts on multi-tools, knives, cutting tools, and other equipment.
- GORUCK: 15 percent military discount to active and retired US armed forces members
- Grand Targhee Resort: US military personnel with a valid ID can purchase lift tickets for $45.
- Jack Frost Big Boulder Resort: Military discount on lift tickets
- Jans: Active-duty and retired military members can get a 15 percent discount.
- Jay Peak Resort, Vermont: 50 percent discount on day lift tickets to active-duty US military members. Also eligible for 50 percent off Pump House tickets and 10 percent off regular lodging rates. Season pass is free for those who are deployed in Vermont.
- Leatherman: Active-duty military members can apply to the Leatherman Pro Program for discounts on knives, multi-tools, and other pocket accessories.

- Lite Flight Helicopters: US armed forces members with valid ID can get 50 percent off single-rider tours using the code hero or 10 percent off military group tours
- Loon Mountain Resort, New Hampshire: 10 percent discount on summer/fall activities and up to $10 off lift tickets during winter to current and former US military personnel
- Monarch Mountain: US military members and their dependents are eligible for Military Ticket pricing.
- Ocean Ashes: One free ash scattering service every month to families with a military veteran who has passed away, and 10 percent off ocean ash scattering packages
- Orvis: 10 percent military discount on select purchases to active-duty and retired US armed forces members who apply for Veterans Advantage
- Pat's Peak: US armed forces personnel and their dependents can get $20 off lift tickets Monday to Friday and $15 off during weekends and holidays
- Pico Mountain: Active-duty and retired members of the US military can get a free Killington/Pico Express Card that provides discounted lift tickets and other benefits.
- Shawnee Mountain Ski Area: Discounted lift tickets to active-duty military members
- Spyderco: Veterans and active-duty military personnel can get discounts when they join the OpFocus Professional Purchase Program.
- Sugar Mountain Resort: Discounted slope/lift tickets to active-duty US military personnel, their spouses, and dependent children of age seventeen and below
- Sun & Ski Sports: Active-duty US military personnel and veterans who can provide valid proof of service are eligible for a 10 percent military discount.
- SunnySports: 6 percent military discount on select pur-

chases to current and former US armed forces members and their families

- Tough Mudder: Active-duty, reserve, and retired members of the US armed forces can receive up to 25 percent off registration fees on events
- Wachusett Mountain: Active-duty US military members can buy a special season pass to get $15 off lift ticket prices plus other benefits.
- Whitewater Rafting Adventures: Active and retired members of the US military and National Guard can get 15 percent off admission rates.
- Wildcat Mountain Ski Area: Active-duty and retired military members and their dependents can get a free Military Discount Card so they can save 25 percent on holiday/weekend lift tickets and 40 percent during nonholidays.

CIGARS AND E-CIGARETTES

- Bobalu Cigar Co.: 10 percent military discount to active-duty members of the US armed forces
- Cigars International: Veterans, active-duty military personnel, and military family members can get a 10 percent discount.
- G&R Premium Cigars, Wichita Falls, Texas: Veterans and active-duty military personnel are eligible for military discounts.
- Halo Cigs: Veterans and active-duty US military personnel can get 15 percent off online purchases.
- Holt's Cigar: 10 percent military discount to active and retired members of the US armed forces and National Guard
- JR Cigar: 10 percent military discount on cigar orders shipped to APO and FPO addresses

- JUUL: Active and retired US armed forces members can receive special discounts on e-cigarettes.
- Leaf Affair Cigar Shop: 10 percent military discount to US armed forces personnel
- NH Cigars: Active duty military members and veterans of the US armed forces can qualify for free shipping when they upgrade their account to Veteran status.
- Sheepdog Cigar: Active and retired military personnel can join the club by paying a lifetime membership fee of $75 so they can receive special discounts and benefits.
- Thompson Cigar: 10 percent military discount to active-duty and retired US armed forces members and their families

PARTY AND OCCASION

- 1-800-Flowers: 20 percent discount to active and retired US military service members and their families
- 1st in Flowers: Active-duty military members and their families receive a 15 percent discount.
- Braselton Event Center, North Georgia: Active and retired military personnel can get 10 percent off wedding packages plus free limousine service.
- Brides across America: Free wedding dresses to military brides every year
- From You Flowers: US armed forces members can redeem a 20 percent military discount or free shipping.
- Heartland Meadows, Knoxville, Tennessee,: 10 percent wedding discount to military grooms, brides, or their parents
- Kendall's View: Military couples can get a 10 percent discount on wedding packages.
- Magnolia Grace Ranch, Texas: Military brides and grooms can get 5 percent off wedding day bookings.

- ProFlowers: 15 percent military discount on select purchases by US armed forces members and veterans
- Sugar Beach Weddings: Active members of the US armed forces are eligible for exclusive discounts on select wedding packages.
- The Springs Events: Brides and grooms that are active or veteran members of the US military can get $200 off wedding venue reservations.
- Twin Oaks Guest Ranch: Active or retired US military members can save 10 percent off their wedding reservation.
- Virginia's House, Arizona: Military discounts on wedding packages and venues to members of the US armed forces
- Wedgewood Weddings: Active-duty members of the military get 10 percent off non-Saturday wedding packages.

STORAGE

- 509 Packing and Cleaning: US military personnel in Spokane can get 10 percent off cleaning, packing, and moving services.
- CubeSmart: 10 percent storage discount plus other exclusive benefits to active-duty US armed forces members
- Lowe's: Active and retired US military members can apply for a 10 percent military discount on select products.
- Man Crates: Military families can save 10 percent on select orders.
- PODS: Active US armed forces personnel can get a 10 percent military discount on storage services.
- SMARTBOX: Active-duty military members can receive $20 off moving and storage services.
- uShip: Discounts of up to 61 percent off moving and relocation services to active-duty and retired military, veterans, and military spouses

- Zippy Shell: Variable discount based on location

MILITARY DISCOUNT MEMBERSHIPS

- Armed Forces Vacation Club: Free membership for veterans
- Caesars Rewards: 10 percent discount with no blackout dates
- ID.me/Troop ID: Instant verification of military status to authenticate qualification for military discounts
- LinkedIn: Free one-year access to LinkedIn Premium and LinkedIn Learning
- Military Cost Cutters: Free Loyalty Rewards Program membership
- Theatre Development Fund: Save up to $70 on tickets to musicals and theater shows.

ABOUT THE AUTHOR

I was advised to write a few sentences about myself for the author's bio. My publishing team, family, and friends have all told me, "Delano, let the people know who you are. Tell them your story. Build credibility with your readers." I could tell you that I'm an Enduring Freedom war veteran who served in combat, that I'm a former high school football and basketball coach, that my parents were born in the Bahamas, that I graduated from the University of Miami with honors, that I've owned several businesses and purchased multiple properties, that I love my country and most of all our Lord and Savior, but truthfully none of that matters. This is one of the many reasons I wrote this book. This book is not about who I am, where I'm from, or what I've accomplished. This book is about you; this book is about us; this book is about America. We have become so self-obsessed, so self-absorbed, so self-centered that we have lost our ability to defer, we've lost our ability to reason, we've lost our ability to unite. Everyone knows that there is power in numbers. Unity induces cohesion; cohesion creates strength; strength sustains power. Long story short: it's not about me, it's about us.

Printed in the USA
CPSIA information can be obtained
at www.ICGtesting.com
LVHW050757241223
767218LV00034B/815/J